PLANTS & GARDENS
in TOWNS & CITIES

PLANTS & GARDENS in TOWNS & CITIES

by Stan Larke

Illustrations by Ruth Bagshaw

McGRAW-HILL RYERSON LIMITED

Toronto Montreal New York London Sydney
Johannesburg Mexico Panama Düsseldorf Singapore
São Paulo Kuala Lumpur New Delhi

Plants and Gardens in Towns and Cities

Copyright © McGraw-Hill Ryerson Limited, 1975.
All rights reserved. No part of this publication may be reproduced, stored in a retrieval system, or transmitted in any form or by any means, electronic, mechanical, photocopying, recording, or otherwise, without the prior written permission of McGraw-Hill Ryerson Limited.

Hardcover ISBN 0-07-082233-6
Paperback ISBN 0-07-082247-6

1 2 3 4 5 6 7 8 9 0 THB 4 3 2 1 0 9 8 7 6 5

Printed and bound in Canada by
T. H. Best Printing Company Limited, Don Mills, Ontario

CONTENTS

Introduction 11

Shade 13
Natural Shade
The Soil in the Shade
Growing Vegetables in the Shade
Planting Shade Trees
Shade-tolerant Plants
Vines
Low-growing and Flowering Plants

Slopes and Little Corners 20
Ground Covers on Slopes
Shrubby Plants for Slopes
North Slopes
The Sloping Lot
Those Awkward Corners

Soil That's Dry and Sandy 29
Planting Trees and Shrubs in Sand
Trees for Sandy Places
Shrubs That Thrive in Sand
Perennials for Sandy Soils
Annuals for Sandy Soils

Bog Gardens 34
Bog-loving Shrubs
Bog Trees
Standing Water
Homemade Swamps
How to Drain Wet Areas

Water Gardens 38
Selecting the Location
Water Garden Plants
Cold-zone Water Gardens
Water Lilies

Terraces, Patios & Decks 42
Plants to Enclose the Terrace or Patio
Points of Accent
Don't Waste the Nooks, Cracks and Crannies
Plant Your Own Spring View
Tubs and Containers

The Fragrant Garden *49*
Perfume in the Patio Planters
Plan for Fragrance in the Shrubbery too
Fragrance in a Garden Three Feet Square
The Sweetest of Trees

Floral Paving *53*
Selecting the Floral Paving Plants
The Tufting Plants
The Carpeting Plants
General Care

Apartment Gardens *55*
Watering
Feeding
Remember the Dangers of Frost
Soil for the Containers
Selecting the Planter
Hanging Baskets
Plants that Hang and Trail
House Plants on the Balcony
The Standards
Growing Plants Need Not Be Expensive
Vegetables for the Apartment Gardener
The Container Planting Medium
Fertilizing the Container-held Vegetable Plants
Watering Container-grown Vegetables
Light Requirements
Insect Control
Growing Vegetables the Easy Way

Sunless Gardening *69*
The Fluorescent Fixture
Unusual and Novelty Plants Possible under Lights
Water Gardens Under Lights
Aquarium Gardening Under Lights

Gardening At The Office *74*
Light, Humidity and Temperature are Important
Take Care with Watering
Plants that Tolerate Office Conditions
Plants for Poor Light Conditions
Plants for Drafty Places with Changing Temperatures

Bottle, Terrarium & Dish *77*

Tools *84*
Qualities To Look For In Tools

The Compost Heap *85*
The Small-scale Compost Heap
The Pill
Large Compost Heaps
Using the Compost Material

Mulch *89*
Mulch is a Work Saver
Handling Mulch Materials
Plastic Mulches

Soil *91*
Ideal Soil
Organic Matter is a Must
Good Drainage is Required
Why Bother to Fertilize?
Soil Tests Usually Tells All
Heavy Clay
Soils for Seedlings
Sterilize Your Own Seedling Soil

Start Your Own Seeds *96*
The Old-Fashioned Way
The Modern Way to Start Your Own Seeds
Don't Get Started Too Soon

Cold Frames and Hotbeds *100*
Heating the Garden Frame
Making the Garden Frame
For Those Who Have Plenty of Space
Scalded-down Frames

Rooting Shrub Cuttings *105*
A Miniature, Miniature Propagation Case
When and What to Cut
Some Handy Equipment
The Rooting Medium
Preparing and Planting the Cuttings

Rooting Hardwood Cuttings *108*
When and What to Cut
Rooting the Hardwood Cuttings

From Seeds to Trees *110*
Patience is Needed
Seed Harvest Times
Seeds to Store or Not Store
Seeds Often Need Treatment
Treatment of Seeds for Starting Specific Trees
Results to Expect

Wintering Trees *116*
Provide Protection at the Right Time
Winter Tree Injuries

The Salty City *119*
A Good Way to Melt Snow

Birds, Berries & Peace *121*
Birds and Berries
How to Attract the Birds to Deep Downtown Shade
Grow a Hedge that will Draw Birds and Stop Noise
Enjoy Various Colours of Plants While Feeding Birds
Berries for Birds And for People
Winter Bird-feeding Stations

Tiny Trees and Shrubs *126*
Dwarf Shrubs for Shady Places
Dwarf Shrubs for Sandy Places
Dwarf Shrubs for Normal Conditions
The Versatile Dwarfs
What is a Dwarf Plant?
Smallest and Hardiest Evergreens
Soil for Dwarf Conifers

Crab Trees *131*
Largest Crab Apples
Smallest Crab Apples
Weeping Crab Apples
Hardiest Crab Apples

Grasses for Downtown *132*
Creeping Red Fescue Resists Pollution Best
Seeding New Lawns

Children's Gardens *135*
Indoor Projects for Children

Vegetable Gardens *137*
First Things First: Sun, Rain, Protection
The Soil
The Easy Method
Nutrition in the Soil is Essential
The Garden Layout

Herb Gardens *142*
The Three Main Kinds of Herbs
Herb Garden Layouts

Fall Flowers *145*
Chrysanthemums
Anemone Japonica
Michaelmas Daisies

Cut & Dried Flowers *147*
Caring for Fresh-cut Flowers
How to Cut
When to Cut
Harvest Gourds and Herbs in the Fall
Drying Herbs
Dried Flowers for Everlasting Bouquets
Air Drying
Silica Gel Crystals

Overrun Gardens *150*
Don't Just Dig and Destroy
The Time to Dig
The Logic of the Plan
Prune 'em Back Alive

Lilacs New & Old *153*
Dwarf Lilac
Most Common Lilac
When and What to Plant
Care After Planting
Care of Established Lilacs

INTRODUCTION

How many times have you heard people say "I just can't grow anything, because I don't have space," or "I don't have time for gardening—I'm much too busy." In this book I will show you that there is really no reason why everyone cannot live among friendly, growing plant life.

This book is for people with space problems, environment problems, time problems. It is for the ninety-nine per cent of us who don't have a country estate. I'll show how people who live in one room without a balcony or even a windowsill can relax with colourful, fragrant, and even exotic flowers around them. I'll describe balcony gardens and window planters and hanging baskets. I'll introduce you to patio planters and raised beds and basement and attic gardening. I'll list trees and shrubs and plants that will thrive in places that have been considered wasteland.

Growing vegetables is becoming increasingly popular for many reasons. High food costs and concern about nutrition have started many people growing their own. I'll talk about growing vegetables in small spaces, in shady spots, even in containers indoors and out. There is really no mystery to it.

There is an ecological side to this book as well. Nature, left to her own devices, wastes nothing, and all the leaves and dead plants and other debris that fall to the ground are broken down to form the topsoil. Every handful of topsoil is teeming with vital life that is an essential part of the life cycle. It is up to us to do our part to replenish the precious topsoil by recycling organic materials. That is why I am so keen on compost heaps.

Everyone should be aware of nature's basic method of production. When sunlight strikes the outer surface of living plants, the miracle of photosynthesis occurs, transforming the vital energy of the sun into usable commodities in the form of glucose, heat and vital gases without which nothing on earth could survive. Every parking lot, highway and building represents less space for oxygen-producing green plans to grow in. It is up to us to make up for the asphalt jungle by growing plants wherever we can.

Stan Larke

SHADE

Downtown or in the suburbs, the gardener is sure to be faced with the problem of shade. Downtown the problem is likely to be too much shade, from neighbouring buildings, fences or mature trees. In the suburbs, especially in new developments, there may be too little shade and the gardener will have to plant trees strategically and erect trellises and so forth to provide protection from the sun.

Take notice of the patterns of shadow and sunlight in the woods on a sunny day. Using shade to your advantage, the garden can be an almost psychedelic picture of form and colour with various leaf and bark textures and shapes.

There are some flowering annual plants, herbaceous perennials with good foliage and flowers, and vines, shrubs and trees with desirable features that actually thrive in various kinds of shade. Once you've become familiar with these shade-loving plants, the shade on your property need never be a problem again. Even some of our brightest-coloured annual flowers will put on a fabulous show in the shade—violas (including pansies), many varieties of petunias, fibrous-rooted begonias and others.

There is always one side of the house, or one section of the garden, or some little corner demanding plants that will tolerate living conditions in the shade of trees, a roof overhang, or tall buildings.

Deep shade is found on the north side of a building where the sun never shines, medium shade on the north-east side where the sun shines for about an hour in the morning. Checkered shade may be found under small-leaved trees such as the honey-locust.

Before solving the problem of what to plant in the shade on your property, you must first determine the kind of shade you have. Is it the permanent kind of heavy shade that is found on the north side of the building or between two buildings? Is it the medium-to-heavy shade beneath tall trees? Is it the kind of shade that is there for only part of the day, or only part of the year? Is it planned shade?

Natural Shade

Nature's plan includes shade. Nature plants her forests (including the shade) in the following manner. The leafy crowns of the tallest trees make up what is called the canopy. Often the tall trees are widely spaced and the canopy is open, allowing a lot of sunshine to penetrate through to the layers below. Where the tallest trees grow close together with their branches interweaving, the canopy becomes closed as though it were a huge canvas shutting out sunlight and making dense shade. Whether the canopy is open or closed, many types of plants will still flourish in the lower layers.

Down from the tall trees of the canopy we come to the understory, the medium-sized trees, some of which will eventually take their place among the canopy although many may perish before finding the opening needed for an upward thrust. Below the understory is the shrub layer: woody plants that have several stems.

Beneath the shrub layer is the herb layer of plants, those that have soft, rather than woody, stems. Most wild flowers and grasses are herbs. Ferns, mushrooms and mosses that grow close to the ground also make up the herb layer.

Very careful studies of the understory and the shrub layers of many forest areas have given our modern experts much valuable information about which trees and shrubs can withstand living in the shade.

If you intend to cultivate plant life (be it a ground cover or another tall tree) in the shade on your property, make certain that the material you buy is known to be shade-tolerant. Local nurserymen will know which varieties have been proven in your area.

Begonias in a built-up bed in a shady spot: logs, timbers, railway ties, stones or other materials will retain the soil.

The Soil in the Shade

The soil is the most important factor when planting in the shade. In shade, the soil is often infested with the roots of large trees from the neighbourhood, and may be completely devoid of nutrition. If this is the case, not even straggly grasses will grow. Shaded soil must be given good drainage and plenty of plant food. This particular requirement is often easily met by constructing a raised bed in which to grow your plants. Raised beds are usually surrounded by some sort of structural form that makes a suitable enclosure for fresh soil. When your receptacle is built—usually at very low cost from any number of materials that are readily available, such as railroad ties, concrete blocks, building stone—fill it with good rich soil and start fresh with your shade gardening from there. When constructing the receptacle, be sure to provide for good drainage so that waterlogging does not occur. Unless they can be made very large and deep, raised beds are not recommended for perennial and woody plants in the coldest areas; annuals, and the bulbuous and tuberous plants which are dug up in the fall and stored indoors are recommended.

If you use the soil that is already there, its acidity should be considered. Shaded soils are often acid and sour and should be made more alkaline and sweetened with charcoal or lime. In order to determine the pH (the acid or alkaline content) of the soil, make simple tests with an inexpensive soil test kit, or have it done by an outside party. If your local nurseryman can't help with the soil test, your local Department of Agriculture representative certainly can and will help you.

You may find that you'd be much further ahead to entirely remove the old soil and replace it with the best you can afford to buy. When removing old soil, be prepared to allow for the protection of roots of trees and shrubs as they must not be allowed to remain high and dry for even a few minutes. Cover them with wet burlap or wet peat moss or some other such material, and be sure to keep those roots covered during the soil exchange.

Growing Vegetables in the Shade

More often than not the gardener who lives in the crowded conditions of towns and cities must do his gardening in places that cannot be considered ideal. We've all seen those little bits of unpaved areas that run under the speckled shade of a metal fire escape, that tiny patch of soil next to a building at the back door of a downtown structure where we usually see forgotten paint cans and other discarded junk. These little places, that appear as if barely-missed by being covered over by pavement, can often be converted from neglected eyesores into miniature gardens of Eden.

Such plants as vines and climbers, shade-tolerant trees and shrubs and foliage plants can all be coaxed to stretch themselves upwards towards the sky even from abandoned concrete stairwells. Vegetables are a different matter.

Vegetables require a certain amount of sunlight; ideally a minimum of six hours sunlight per day will suffice to keep a vegetable garden healthy and productive. I do not suggest that any gardener try growing vegetables in a totally shaded area, knowing that he or she would be in for disappointment. However, if in these cul-de-sacs at least two to four hours of daily sunlight is available, it is quite possible to baby-along some vegetables. I'd suggest growing the really easy ones such as radishes, green onions, leaf lettuce, beets, and perhaps one or two pole climbers such as beans and peas. The pole climbers will require a minimum amount of space in the soil while all the growth is suspended above on their supports.

To help make these tidbit-sized vegetable gardens produce, they'll have to be given kid-glove treatment right from the beginning. First clear out all the junk and debris that will have gathered over the years. Dig down to a foot in depth and remove all tree roots, rocks, bricks, etc. Since you are dealing with only a very small amount of earth, excavate the entire area. Break up those rocks and bricks and add more small stones or gravel to them and make a layer of coarse drainage material four to six inches deep. Before backfilling the soil that was removed, mix with it several things that will turn that worthless earth into a high-quality growing medium. Make it loose and fluffy and rich in nutrients by adding plenty of organic matter such as peat moss, or perlite. Also mix in some powdered charcoal and composted manure. If it is available, I would also recommend the addition of about an inch of sharp building sand over the entire area, thoroughly mixed in with all the other additives.

When you get the soil for your little garden mixed to the point where you can run your fingers through it and easily poke a stick through from top to bottom, then it is time to add a vegetable fertilizer according to the directions on the package and mix it all thoroughly together.

Move the newly-prepared soil mix back into the excavation. There should be enough to mound it several inches above the original surface. At this point you can apply your artistic skills and build a small retaining wall around the fluffy, new bed using either wood, brick, blocks, stone, logs, timbers, clay tiles, or whatever will fit in with your overall plan for the reclamation of the dingy yard, or even leave it as it is.

Just after the last frost of the spring, sow your vegetable seeds according to directions on the packages, then gently water the area and start looking after it as though it was the last garden patch on earth. Keep it moist, keep it weeded, and keep it fed. It is possible to harvest your first radish in twenty to forty days and your first spinach crop in thirty to sixty days.

Planting Shade Trees

Too much sun may be your problem. You may find you don't have enough shade.

Locating a tree with an eye to the shade it will cast can be tricky, as the sun's rays are almost always shifting the angle at which they strike the property. The sun is in a northward course over North America until June 21st, the longest day of the year, and then it immediately starts a southward course until December 31st, the shortest day of the year.

When a tree is planted on the south property line, it will have an almost straight-down shadow in June giving little more shade than the

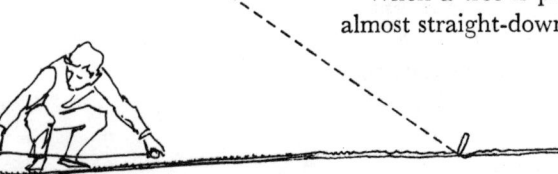

Measure the shadow cast by a pole of known length. The shadow of a tree in the same spot will be in the same proportion to its height as the pole's shadow—if the tree is three times as high as the pole, its shadow will be three times as long.

area of its branch spread; in August, the same tree will cast a long, north-stretched shadow. A tree planted on the north property line will never cast a shadow on your property any larger than the diameter of the branch spread. This is a good fact to remember when giving consideration to the shade your trees will cast on the neighbours' gardens.

Consider also the purpose of the shade that will be cast by the tree. Will it provide an air-conditioning effect on the house? Will it create a soft, lacy, half-bright light such as under a honey locust? Will it make a dense shade so dark that under it nothing will grow (such as under a hard maple)? When planted in the right places, shade trees can cool the barbeque area and patio by as much as 10 degrees. Obviously in mid-summer this cooling effect can mean the difference between sweltering or enjoying a summer's day. Trees can also be located so that they shade the house at the right time of day, cooling the outside walls and reducing the temperature inside.

Consider slanting rays of the sun plus the knowledge that the hottest part of the day is between 3:00 and 5:00 p.m. in making the decision as to where a shade tree should be planted. Make sure that the shade will be sufficient to protect the roof and wall of the house, or the patio, from those late afternoon slanting rays. This is done by planting your tree twenty to twenty-five feet to the west of the area to be shielded. If cooler mornings are desired on the east side of the house, plant a tree twenty to twenty-five feet to the east of the area to be shaded.

If the outdoor living area is located on the east side of the house, only the overhead noonday sun need be screened off as the shadow of the house will give shade in the afternoon and evening. When the outdoor living area is situated on the west side of the house, two shade trees will be required; one located twenty to twenty-five feet to the west, which will block the hot afternoon slanting rays, and the other in a position to make shade under the overhead noonday sun.

If a tree is to provide shade immediately after planting, a fairly large one, at least fifteen to sixteen feet tall, will have to be planted. Trees of this size, container-held, or wrapped with a good rootball, can be planted in the spring. Large size trees, sixteen to nineteen feet and taller are better moved in the winter or very early spring. If the average six to eight foot tree is planted (the most common size), expect a waiting period of seven to ten years before enough growth is produced to make good shade.

The shade of evergreen trees can be more of a problem than that of deciduous trees. In early spring, deciduous trees cast very little shade, allowing the spring-flowering bulbs and perennials to flower and run their growth cycle before shade becomes too dense. On the other hand, evergreens often cause so much shade that nothing will grow under their branches. Evergreens, planted along a path or driveway, will hold ice and snow long after all other parts of the garden have begun spring drying, which can be bothersome and messy.

Shade-tolerant Plants

The following is a list of suggested planting stock for growing areas of shade or very little light. Please remember that these are only suggestions and should not be considered as the entire selection of such plants.

TREES IN DEEP SHADE   The hop hornbeam (*Ostrya virginiana*) is a natural understory tree.

Blue beech (*Carpinus caroliniana* var. *virginiana*). This tree is often hard to find on the market, but when a search is sincerely made it can usually be found.

Striped maple (*Acer pennsylvanicum*) will produce striped green bark and large light-green leaves in shade when given a good rich soil and good drainage.

TREES IN MEDIUM SHADE   Allegheny shadbush (*Amelanchier laevis*) is particularly colourful in early spring, especially in Eastern areas.

Black cherry (*Prunus serotina*) has, like all cherries, attractive bark texture plus early spring foliage.

Sugar maple (*Acer saccharum*) has all the familiar maple features including good autumn colour.

Where the soil is poor, the European white birch (*Betula pendula*) and the maidenhair tree (*Ginkgo biloba*) are two suggested tree varieties that are well-suited to these conditions.

SHRUBS IN DEEP SHADE   Snowhill Hydrangea (*Hydrangea arborescens* 'Grandiflora') bears huge trusses of white flowers in August and September. The new member of this family called 'Annabelle' is especially desirable.

Alpine currant (*Ribes alpinum*) is a good specimen shrub for deep shade, where it also makes a good hedge plant.

All members of the yew family of evergreens will survive in shade. The very hardy Japanese yew (*Taxus cuspidata*) will thrive and produce their familiar bright-red berries when shrubs of both sexes are planted.

Creeping wintercreeper (*Euonymus fortunei* 'Carrierei') will transform a dark corner of the property into a blaze of fall colour and provide interesting contrasts all year round.

Snowberry (*Symphoricarpos albus* 'Laevigatus') will produce an abundance of brilliant, white berries even in very heavy shade.

SHRUBS IN MEDIUM TO LIGHT SHADE *Pachistima canbyi* is one of the broadleaved evergreens which can tolerate light shade (given about an hour of sun at either end of the day). It forms a short, dense, dark-green bush twelve to eighteen inches in height. The Oregon grape (*Mahonia aquifolium*) features good foliage colour, with leaves shaped like holly, and also produces yellow flowers and blue fruit. The Mezereon shrubs are available with both white and rose-pink forms.

The dwarf, highbush cranberry and the dwarf cultivars of *Skogholm Cotoneaster* will grow in light shade.

Vines

The vine that flowers profusely in shade is the climbing hydrangea (*Hydrangea petiolaris*); it has been available to gardeners for many years but is now enjoying a great comeback. This climbing hydrangea clings strongly to brick walls and does best on a north or east wall, but should be given a location protected against frigid winter blasts. Virginia creeper (*Parthenocissus quinquefolia*) is another good selection.

For growing on a western wall or in half-shade you may choose from bittersweet (*Celastrus scandens*), Boston ivy (*Parthenocissus tricuspidata lowii*), or Dutchman's pipe (*Aristolochia durior*).

Low-growing and Flowering Plants

You might take a look at the varieties of plants that grow in deep shade in the wild for clues to which low-growing plants thrive in the deepest shade. Such ferns as New York fern, lady fern, and the maidenhair fern, all do well when they are provided with a good, rich, peaty soil. Lily-of-the-valley, and plantain lilies (*Hosta* species), the hepaticas, and wild ginger with its pale-green leaves, also thrive in deep shade.

Some of the plants that produce attractive flowers in the shade include Solomon's seal (*Polygonatum multiflorum*) which also features bright-green leaves, and Virginia cowslip (*Mertensia virginica*).

Two of the better known ground covers—plants that replace grass—include Japanese spurge (*Pachysandra terminalis*) and periwinkle (*Vinca minor*).

Bulbous plants that seem to prefer shade are Siberian squills and daffodils.

Some of the annuals that offer great displays of colour are impatiens, coleus, and begonias.

SLOPES AND LITTLE CORNERS

Very often the purchaser of a newly-built home in a recently-opened area is faced with the problem of what to do with the ditch left across the front or back of the lot as a storm drain until underground services are installed. Frequently these slope-sided ditches almost become permanent features of the landscape, often remaining for several years, and so must be dealt with.

Unquestionably, the easiest way to handle slopes is to sow or sod grass. Grass is the answer if the slope is on a grade gentle enough to allow for easy mowing and maintenance; otherwise, other plants called ground covers must be brought in. It should never be forgotten that the ditch does serve an important function and nothing should be done to restrict its ability to handle a flow of water.

In cases where the home owner prefers to seed the slope to grass, he should first try to grade the sides for a minimum slope. The surface should be smoothed and then seeded with the following suggested seed mixture: equal parts of red fescue; Kentucky bluegrass; and perennial rye grass. The fast-germinating rye grass will hold the soil together until the other two varieties get a good, firm grip. After sowing, cover the seeded area with material, such as burlap, in order to prevent the soil being washed away down the slope.

Remove the fabric covering just as soon as germination starts. When the grasses on the sides of the ditch have become rooted, go ahead and sow the ditch area at the bottom to finish the job. Autumn is when nature sows her seeds and also seems to be the best time for man to follow her example. However, if the seedbed is kept moist, by continually and lightly watering the burlap covering over the seed, grasses sown in spring or early summer should be just as hardy as fall-sown grass.

The laying of sod can be done any time from early spring to late fall provided the soil is not frozen hard. The sods need to be tamped firmly into place, secured with wooden pegs which can be cut from small tree branches, and then drenched with water regularly until they are well-rooted and have a good grip on the slope.

Ground Covers on Slopes

If you have decided that there is no hope of growing grass on your slopes, there are many other forms of plant life than can be planted to stop the soil from eroding. Remember that grass is the best of all ground covers, but the angle of the slope, or the soil on the slope may simply be unsuitable for grass cultivation.

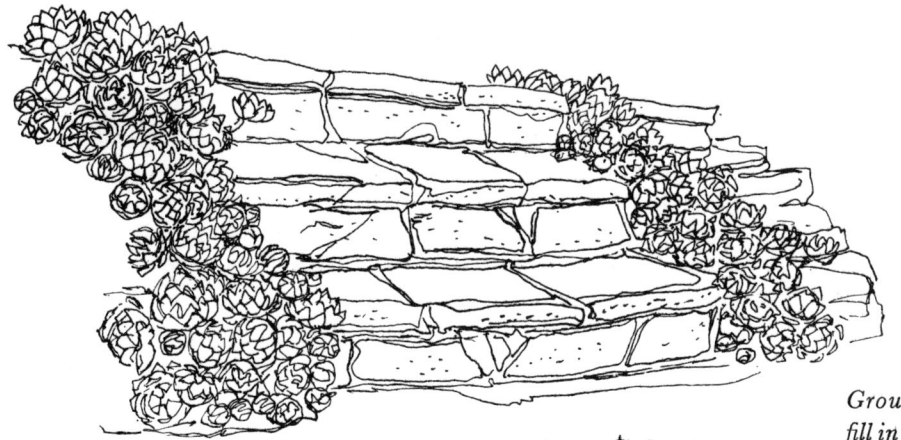

Sempervivum tectorum
(Hens and Chickens)

Ground cover can be used to fill in awkward spaces around steps and pathways and to cover slopes.

If the slope is extremely steep the first part of the solution to the problem is to erect some sort of permanent water barrier up at the top rim, to prevent the flooding which can wash out deep ruts or whole sections of soil. This water barrier need not be at all complicated. Sometimes a small ridge of crushed stone just a few inches deep, or a line of blocks or bricks, or logs or railway ties will make enough of a dam to hold back the torrent of water that rushes over the top during storms. If it is not possible to erect a small wall as described, even the digging of a shallow ditch along the top of the ridge will steer the water away into an area where it won't cause erosion. Remember, if storm-swollen water is allowed to rush down the slope after it is planted with ground covers, you not only lose topsoil but you may also lose the plants during each downpour.

Plants that are classed as, or can be used as, ground covers generally come in one of two types; small, prolific, ground-hugging, creeping plants which actually form a matting over the soil (even under the most adverse conditions); or creeping types of various shrubs, both evergreen and deciduous.

Where the slope tends to be dry and shaded, Japanese spurge (*Pachysandra terminalis*) will thrive. This plant produces many leaves but its flowers are not significant.

The slope that receives a few hours of sunlight per day could sustain some of the ground-matting plants such as creeping phlox or moss pinks (*Phlox subulata*), creeping thyme (*Thymus serpyllum*), dianthus, sedums, or, ground ivy (*Nepeta hederacea*), or snow-in-summer (*Cerastium tomentosum*).

If the slope is of a sandy texture and receives open sunshine all day, the sedums—stonecrops, and sempervivums—hen and chicks, will soon cover the ground with thick, rubbery-leaved plants. Good also in these conditions is the extremely hardy, native bearberry (*Arctostaphylos uva-ursi*) which can be found growing wild far into Canada's northland. It's dark purple foliage is quite attractive.

All of the above mentioned ground covers for slopes can be planted in masses of one individual kind, or can be mixed together to make a very interesting slope texture. As for their care, see that they are weeded until they grow close enough together to crowd out all other growth, after which no further weeding is necessary. Clean out the collected debris, dead parts and straggly growth in the spring and no other special care will be needed.

A wall garden can be an attractive way to cope with a change of levels.

Snow in Summer
Moss Pink
Sempervivum

Shrubby Plants for Slopes

You will notice that when nature plants a slope with shrubs she will very often use the silver-grey and various shades of green of the creeping junipers to do the job with class. Some of the most recommended junipers for this purpose are: a good creeper with dark green foliage is the Wapiti juniper (*Juniperus horizontalis* 'Wapiti'). Blue foliage is available with the Waukegan juniper (*Juniperus horizontalis* 'Douglasii'). Silver foliage is the feature of the Bar Harbor juniper (*Juniperus horizontalis* 'Glauca'). A dense, low-grower that forms a thick, blue carpet over a slope is the blue rug juniper (*Juniperus horizontalis* 'Wiltonii'). The Andorra juniper (*Juniperus horizontalis* 'Plumosa') remains blue all summer and turns purple in the autumn.

Another suggested shrub for slope planting is the Canby pachistima (*Pachistima canbyi*) which grows about eight to ten inches tall and spreads over a wide area.

For a real show, those front lawn storm drainage ditches can be turned into a scene of colour and character with Farrer's shrubby cinquefoil (*Potentilla parvifolia* 'Farreri'). This shrub produces masses of yellow flowers all through the growing season; the foliage turns bronzy in the fall.

North Slopes

When the slope faces the north, although it may receive enough moisture, a plant that requires very little light is needed for effective ground covering. The almost perfect plant, and the most used, is periwinkle, also called myrtle (*Vinca minor*). This blue-flowered plant requires clipping attention only at the edges to keep it within bounds. Plant propagators have now developed new varieties with very large flowers, and those with double-blue and double-plum coloured flowers.

Nursery catalogues suggest many other plants for slope planting.

Many tufting plants are available, such as verbena, sweet alyssum, and small herbs.

Planting wall should lean back 1 inch for each foot of height.

The Sloping Lot

Ground covers are not the only way to treat a slope. The sloping lot offers endless possibilities to create terraces, rock gardens, wall gardens and so forth, using techniques suggested elsewhere in this book. The multi-level garden has an added element of visual interest and is a challenge to any gardener.

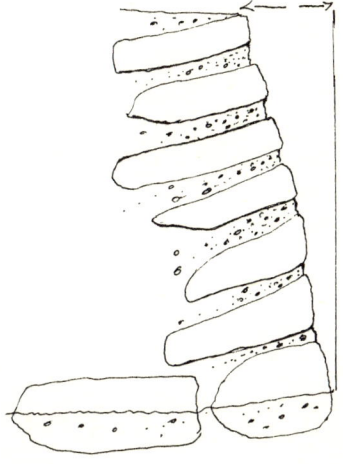

Even the smallest back door space can be brightened up with hanging baskets, containers and trellis.

Those Awkward Corners

Ask any person who tries to grow things in towns and cities and you will hear about dozens of situations that cause problems. This is one time when necessity becomes the mother of invention. Take a look at some of the innovations other downtown gardeners have introduced in order to defeat a problem area and you will be astounded at their resourcefulness.

Let's take the simple, old-fashioned trellis. A trellis can be made to stand upright in a space four inches wide (when fastened to a firmly placed two-by-two inch stake). Also, it can support all manner of space-saving climbing plants, from roses to sweet peas and flowering vines. It can be used, placed tightly against an unsightly wall, to fill the gap between two structures. A trellis could connect the roof overhang with a patio floor or provide privacy in a crowded area. The uses for such

A trellis fills in space between buildings, or any place where a screen or privacy is needed.

plant supports as trellises are numberless. A determined gardener with crowded growing conditions could find even new uses for this helpful contrivance.

Whether you want to surround yourself with growing plants on a balcony, or turn a few square feet of gloom behind a downtown building into a private haven, you can do it with some planning and work. I will guarantee that, if you have a difficult problem place to "do something" with, one trip to a well-stocked, modern, garden center will provide you with many answers.

Vine growing on hinged trellis allows for easy building maintenance.

A small bed of spring bulbs in a sunny corner

Espaliering is a technique of training trees or shrubs to grow flat against a wall, fence or trellis or along wires. Especially useful in constricted situations, it can be a beautiful way of covering an eyesore or making use of an otherwise blank wall. Dwarf form fruit trees or evergreens, such as juniper or euonymus, are suited to this technique. A pear or peach tree trained against the south-facing wall of a house will be both attractive and productive.

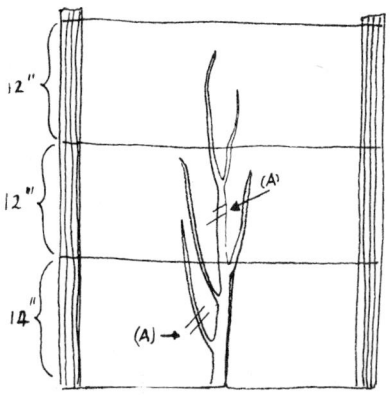

1. On a stout means of support training wires should be set 12 inches apart. Start training the young tree upon planting; the first tier is formed by the two branches at the lowest wire.

A Cut back to leave 3 well placed branches or buds

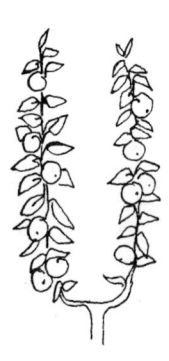

Espaliered in single U form

Espaliered in large 6-arm form

2. Gradually bring branches from the bottom tier into a horizontal position and straighten upright growth. Don't force or damage may result.

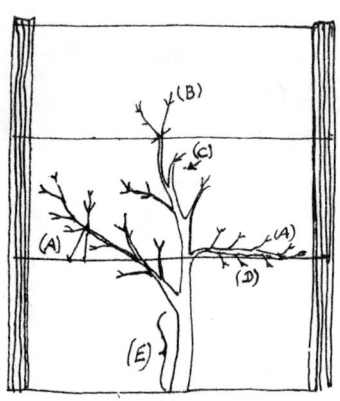

A Tie first tier branches at 45° angle, then gradually bring into horizontal position
B Tie vertical branch to support
C Pinch out lateral tips
D Don't pinch out first tier laterals
E Remove all trunk growth

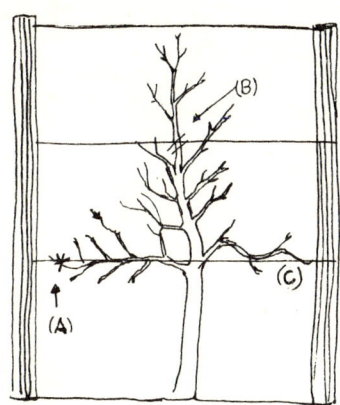

3. During *first* dormant season cut back the vertical branches below the second wire and prune the horizontal growth.

A Tie branch tips to support
B Cut back and re-tie
C Prune terminals only for balance

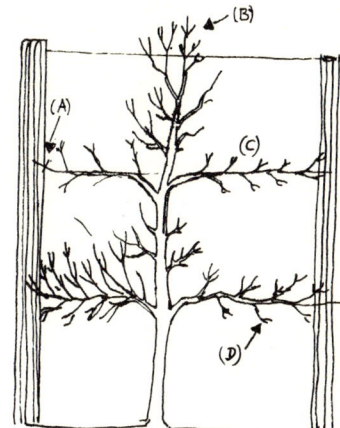

A Tie branch tips to support
B Cut back and re-tie
C Second tier laterals pruned
D First tier lateral side shoots shortened

5. During the second dormant *season*, vertical branches are cut back below the third wire. Second tier laterals are also pruned at this time as with lowest wire the previous year. Follow the same procedure every year to keep new growth under control.

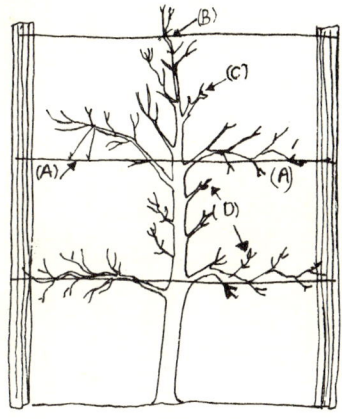

4. In the *second* growing season, train the branches at the second wire as was done on the lowest wire.

A Train second tier branches
B Tie vertical to support
C Pinch out tips of laterals
D Cut back shoots on laterals to 3 buds. Basal buds become fruiting spurs.

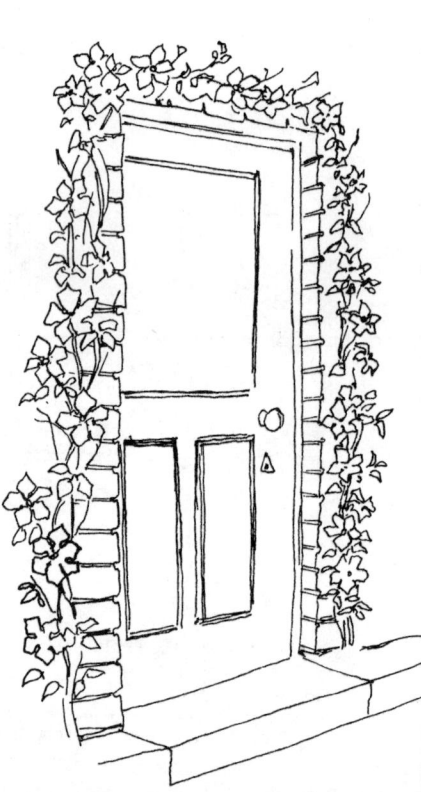

Vines can grow on a single stake or post or along a dowel under an eave.

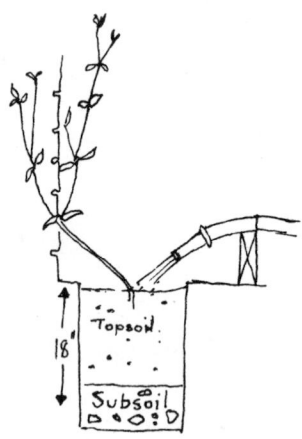

Preparing planting hole for vine. Keep root about nine inches from foundation.

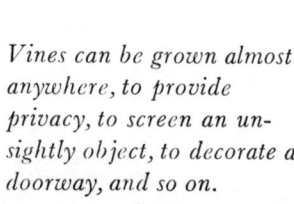

Vines can be grown almost anywhere, to provide privacy, to screen an unsightly object, to decorate a doorway, and so on.

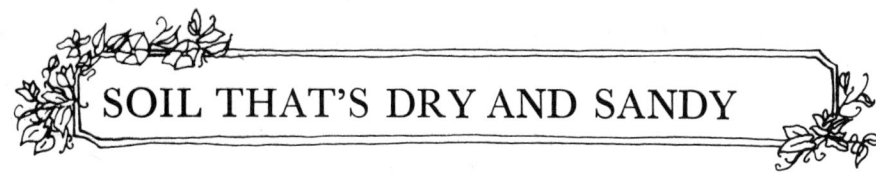
SOIL THAT'S DRY AND SANDY

If the home owner is not faced with areas of dense shade, or wet, soggy soil, or unmanageable slopes, he gets stuck with dry, sandy soil. Most often the soil on city or town properties is the stuff that the contractor dug out of the basement excavation and spread over the lot to save the cost of hauling it away. We can either do the best we can with what we've got or go to the considerable expense or back-breaking work of taking away the old unwanted soil and trucking in new. Or we can select plants that thrive in the existing condition and handle them in the right way.

When working with dry, sandy soils, the soil-conditioning work is exactly opposite to the work done on dense, hard clay soils. With sand, organic material must be added to help retain moisture and plant nutrients; otherwise moisture will just seep away quickly and leave the plants thirsting for food and water.

Some of the recommended organic materials for conditioning the soil include peat moss, leaf mold, garden compost, very well-rotted manure mixed with plenty of straw, and good garden loam. There are many different forms of soil conditioners now available at garden centres which range all the way from perlite and deodorized cow compost to dried sheep manure and baked clay pellets.

Any of the inorganic (man-made types) as well as the organic materials named will do a satisfactory job of retaining moisture in sandy soil. Do not forget that manure in any form should not be considered a complete plant food. Even when heavily manured, sandy soils will require additional fertilizer in order to provide all the plant nutrients needed by the plants.

The important thing to remember about gardening in sandy soils is to get the plants off to a good start. There are many annuals, perennials, shrubs and trees that actually prefer dry, sandy conditions, but only after they have been given a good start. With annual flowers and perennial plants the whole bed area should be improved by working the organic material and plant food into the top ten or twelve inches.

Planting Trees and Shrubs in Sand

When planting trees and shrubs, it is important that the soil be improved with good garden soil and organic matter in the planting holes. Dig the planting hole twice as wide and deep as the soil ball or rootball of the tree or shrub going into it. Half-fill the hole with good topsoil

When planting a tree or shrub in sandy soil, or any other less than satisfactory soil, it is necessary to improve the soil with good garden loam and organic matter.

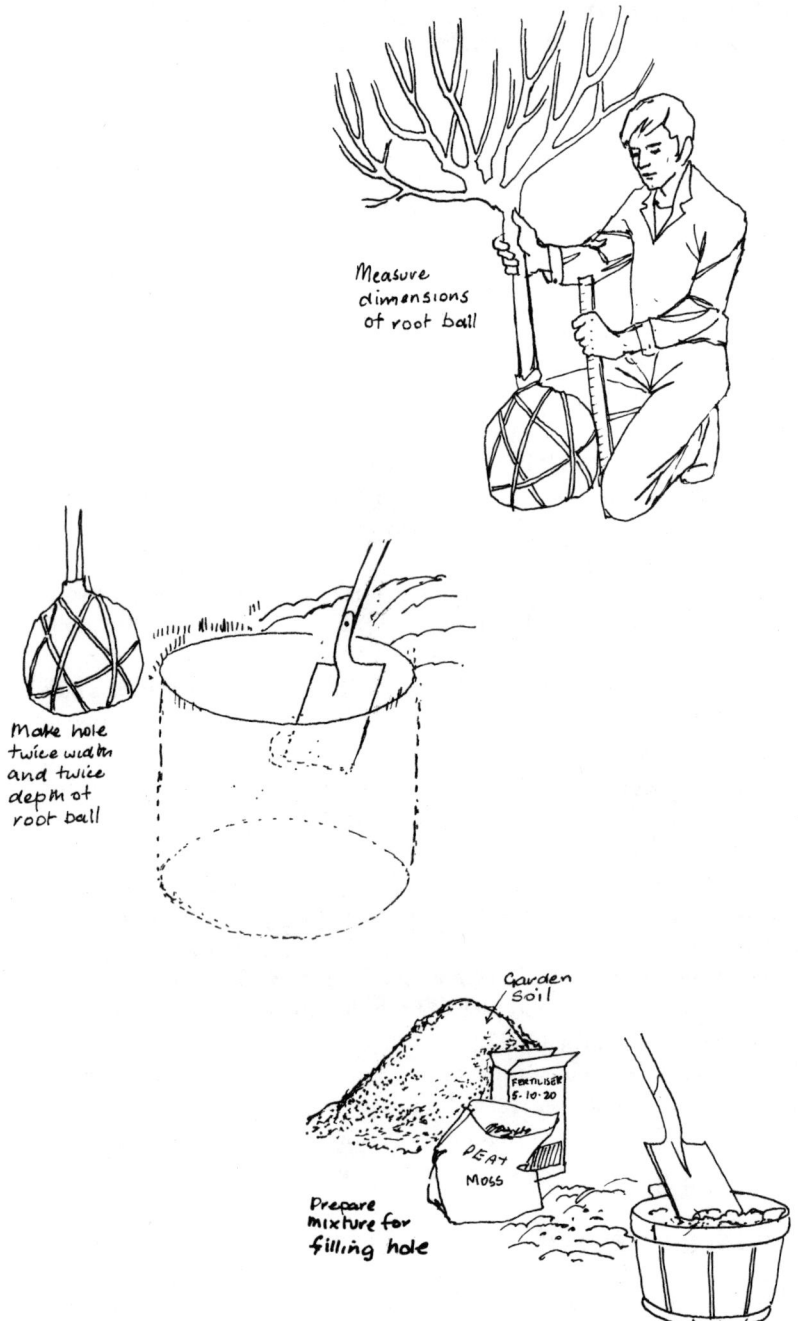

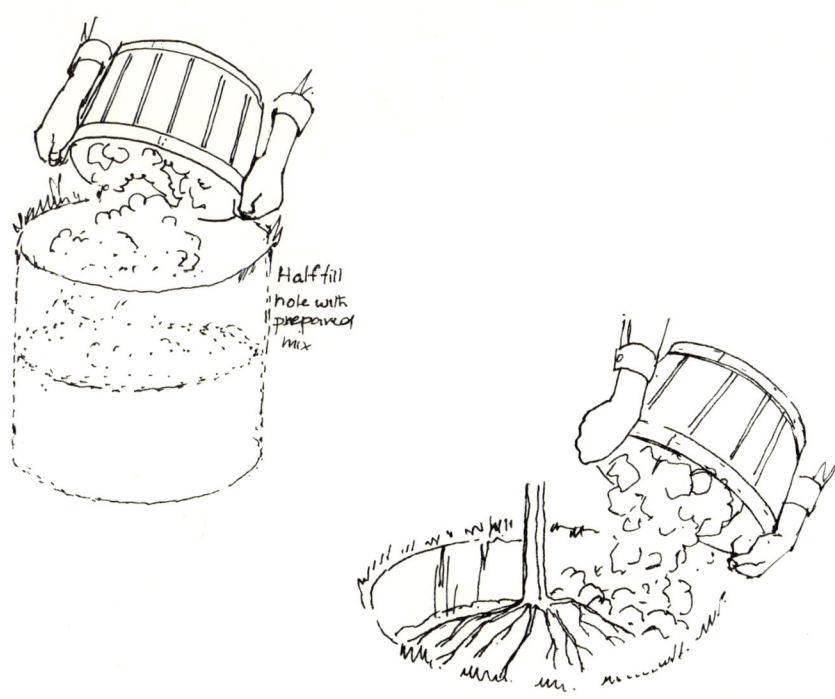

Half fill hole with prepared mix

Set tree in hole to correct depth
Back fill with prepared mixture

Tamp down earth gently.

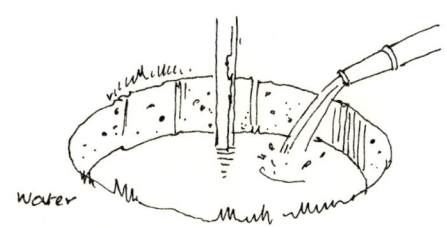

water

Tamp down
Fill hole to near top leaving depression.
Water again

containing lots of organic matter, good garden soil and about a fistful of a balanced fertilizer (5–10–15), all mixed together. Set the tree or shrub in the hole at the correct planting depth (not more than an inch or two below where it previously grew) then backfill around the roots with more of the prepared topsoil mixture. Cover the roots, then gently but firmly tamp down and add water. When the water seeps away, continue backfilling and gently moving the plant back and forth to further settle the soil around the roots and prevent air pockets. Soak with water once more, and then completely backfill the hole leaving a saucer of of space to hold water. Mulch over the whole area with a good mulch material to hold the moisture in the soil by preventing evaporation, and keep the area well-watered until the plant becomes established.

Trees for Sandy Places

I suggest that the Scotch pine (*Pinus sylvestris*) is the best tree to plant in those very dry places. It will quickly grow to thirty to thirty-five feet in twelve to fifteen years. Scotch pine has very few bad qualities except, perhaps, like all pines, it will shed many needles annually.

The most common drawback of trees that thrive in dry, sandy locations is that, while they are very fast growers, they often have very brittle wood. This brittleness makes them vulnerable to wind and ice damage. These trees also shed bark and small branches and twigs. Even so, they will grow in otherwise forgotten places providing shade and attractive colour.

The black locust (*Robinia pseudoacacia*), being a very fast grower, will shoot up to fifteen feet in a mere five years. This tree sprouts suckers abundantly and should not be planted near borders as the suckers will invade the shrubs and become a real nuisance. When planted in an area that is continually mowed or otherwise maintained and where suckers are kept down, the black locust is an ideal fast-growing shade tree for extremely poor growing conditions.

The Siberian elm (*Ulnus pumila*), also commonly called Chinese elm, will quickly grow up to thirty feet in eight to ten years and seems to be the answer to all the gardener's problems. But all is not what it seems. This elm must be pruned at planting time to remove the rival leading shoots. If left on and allowed to grow, these will produce a very weak crotch at the base which will have to be cabled to prevent splitting; or one of the main upright branches must be removed, which would ruin the whole purpose of the tree (that of screening out a bad view, or screening in some privacy). Careful pruning of these competing leaders, and also the strong basal shoots, at planting time are necessary to prevent such problem as split crotches or other damage. The Siberian elm also has the untidy habit of producing a heavy supply of seeds in June which seem to endlessly cover the garden and lawns. This tree is susceptible to the dreaded Dutch elm disease, but to a lesser extent than our native elms which have been destroyed by the million.

Shrubs That Thrive in Sand

Several members of the broom family of shrubs will take to either a sandy slope or an open sandy area with equal vigor. All very hardy brooms are: Portuguese broom (*Cytisus albus*); Golden carpet broom (*Cytisus beani* 'Golden Carpet'), purple broom (*Cytisus purpureus*); spike broom (*Cytisus nigricans*). Although not as hardy, the fabulous Warminster broom (*Cytisus praecox*) performs wonderfully where it can be provided with a sheltered place on a southern outlook.

Some of the cotoneasters will thrive, offering their beautiful thick foliage and colourful fruit, even in poor soils. Varieties to choose for sandy places include: Diels' cotoneaster (*Cotoneaster dielsiana*); Peking cotoneaster (*Cotoneaster acutifolia*); Skogholm cotoneaster (*Cotoneaster dammeri* 'Skogholm'); and rock spray cotoneaster (*Cotoneaster horizontalis*). Other flowering shrubs for sandy areas include several varieties of flowering quince (*Chaenomeles*), and Dyer's greenweed (*Genista tinctoria*).

The inexpensive evergreen junipers of various kinds are ideal plants for sandy slopes. Those such as the Bar Harbor, Wapiti, Waukegan, and Andorra all make excellent ground covers. Other good ground covers for the sandy places are Reynout knotweed (*Polygonum cuspidatum* 'Compactum'), and the yellow sedum (*Sedum acre*).

Perennials for Sandy Soils

Of the perennial class of plants (those that die down to ground level in the fall but remain alive underground to sprout afresh in the spring), varieties having thick roots, or rhizomes, or having thick leaves seem to be the best choices for planting in the sandy places. Some of these plants include: the daylilies in many varieties and colours; gaillardias, known as the blanket flower of the prairies; oriental poppy, which seems to be at its very best in well-drained sand; irises in many varieties; sedums and sempervivums, the hens and chickens. The small soapwood yucca (*Yucca glauca*) of the Arizona desert is quite hardy and will thrive in most of Canada on sandy slopes and dry sandy areas.

Annuals for Sandy Soils

When annuals (those plants that are planted, grow to flower, and die in one season) are planted in sandy areas, some organic matter should be added to the soil to keep in moisture and plant food. In very dry soils you may select from the many varieties of the following plants: cleome; celosia; California poppy; coreopsis; alyssum; portulaca; marigold; and ice plant.

All the above annuals can be grown directly, from seed sown in the area where they are to grow for the season. Provide gentle watering until germination occurs. Seeds can also be started indoors and planted out as transplants, or bedding plants can be purchased and transplanted into the permanent bed.

BOG GARDENS

I don't suppose there are many gardeners living in the densely-populated downtown areas of our towns and cities that have a wetland situation, but I know that many suburban and rural dwellers do. Home gardeners who have permanently wet places on their property should rejoice. Used to the best advantage, bog gardening has taken on such impetus that gardeners are actually spending money to create artificial, bog-like conditions.

Some people are so enthused about water gardening that they sink old bathrubs, and other such receptacles into the ground and proceed as though they had a small pond. Given the right location, this same bog gardening could be enjoyed by downtown gardeners too. (There is a section on the subject of water gardening further on in the text). Water gardening, however, is not quite the same as making the best of a wet, soggy area. When you look carefully through the catalogues you will soon discover things to grow that actually prefer wet conditions.

One of the best examples, of a bog-loving plant that may be used to the best advantage, is the Japanese iris, which is considered to be much more beautiful than the ordinary garden iris. The flower heads of the water-dwelling Japanese irises are often fully eight inches across! Conditions similar to those of a rice paddy are sometimes specially prepared for the purpose of growing these Japanese irises.

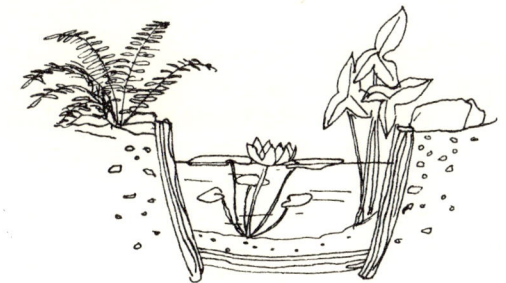

A sunken tub makes a small bog garden. Some plants thrive at the water's edge.

Other perennials that prefer soggy soil include the astilbes, with their many-coloured flowers that last nearly all summer; the garden loosestrifes also enjoy wet feet. So does the yellow-flowering creeping jennie or the money plant (*Lysimachia nummularia*).

Some of the annual plants that prefer wet beds include the monkey flower (*Mimulus*), which sometimes even survives the winter and grows on for another year. A snapdragon-like flower in almost unimaginable colours, the annual hybrid toadflax (*Linaria*), thrives in wet places. Although the impatiens plant (*Impatiens*) is almost always grown in shady places, it will also do extremely well in wet areas, whether in shade or sunshine. Reynoutria fleeceflower (*Polygonum cuspidatum* 'compactum') will grow for you under the very worst conditions.

There are also many shrubs and trees, (some of them our largest-growing trees), that live well in these wet, bog-like areas—a fact which dispells forever the notion that such sections of property need be ignored or hidden behind a fence or wall.

When the gardener prefers to plant shrubs or trees instead of flowering perennials and annuals, see the suggestions listed below.

Bog-loving Shrubs

The buttonbush (*Cephalanthus occidentalis*)
Chokeberries (*Aronia melanocarpa*)
Highbush cranberry (*Viburnum trilobum*)
Dogwoods (*Cornus*)
Sweet pepperbush (*Clethra alnifolia*)
Pusseywillows—only those which do not grow into large trees—goat willow (*Salix caprea*), or French pussywillow, with its pink flowers
Partridgeberry (*Mitchella repens*), which produces edible fruit

Sometimes a whole bog area can be filled to capacity by planting one Sekko willow (*Salix sachalinensis* 'Sekko'). Its twisted and twirled, club-shaped branches make an interesting, curious formation.

Bog Trees

For those who have a lot of space to work with, plant the Golden weeping willow (*Salix alba* 'Tristis'), the pin oak (*Quercus palustris*). Hemlock (*Tsuga canadensis*) and the beautiful red maple (*Acer rubrum*) are also good possibilities.

Standing Water

Places on the property where water actually remains standing on the surface and where improved drainage is impossible, should be treated as ponds and come under the classification of water gardening. However, some plants prefer these particular conditions. Among these are: arrowhead (*Sagittaria latifolia*); flowering rush (*Butomus umbellatus*); and flag flowers (*Iris pseudocorus*).

Whether homemade or natural, bogs seem to thrive equally well in some sun and some shade. Densely-shaded bogs would require a great deal of care in selecting plants to be grown.

Homemade Swamps

If the home gardener is equipped to do so, he can turn a wet area into a man-made swamp and then begin enjoying the beauty of true swamp-growing plants and flowers, many of which are breathtaking in their size, colour and shape. Natural swamps usually feature much decaying vegetation which is rich in plant food, an almost essential factor if swamp plants are to be grown.

Beautiful flowers can be seen as early as April when the golden-yellow marsh marigolds produce their flowers. The wild variety is named (*Caltha palustris*); however, you may prefer to grow the man-handled and refined double variety now on the market. The pitcher plant (*Sarracenia purpurea*) features hollow, pitcher-like leaves which catch insects, as does the interesting plant called the sundew. The cardinal flower (*Lobelia cardinalis*) puts on an astounding show of red in the fall. The jewelweed (*Impatiens biflora*) produces flowers that glisten and have a trigger-like action in the stamens. For yellow flowers in April, plant the swamp buttercup (*Ranunculus septentrionalis*), and for crimson flowers in July and August, the easy-to-grow swamp milkweed (*Asclepias incarnata*) puts on the spectacular display.

How to Drain Wet Areas

If the suggestions for bog gardening, or even swamp gardening haven't convinced you, or if circumstances dictate that a wet area must be drained, the following information should be of value. Common sense indicates that when water stands on the soil surface, it is because the soil is of such a fine, dense structure (like heavy clay) that water cannot penetrate and seep away. Such soils must be opened, loosened and aerated enough to improve the structure so that water can pass through. Dense soils, such as clay, are improved by adding sharp sand—or cinders, peat moss, or perlite—and any other material that will improve the drainage quality. The quantity of soil additives required depends on the amount of drainage needed in the soggy area.

Sometimes the standing water problem is only a matter of low-lying land that needs to be filled in and brought up to the level of the surrounding grade.

When either improving the structure of the soil, or levelling off does not bring about the desired result, tile drains may be the answer. A bed of weeping tile, radiating out from the wet area, may carry away enough moisture to keep the place dry and workable. Maybe a tile line leading to a lower area or a dry well is the answer. Some experimenting with these methods will likely bring about the cure.

If all else fails and the area must be dried up, the experts of the local municipal offices may have the solution.

Tile drainage will drain a soggy area. Weeping tile are left unsealed and should be placed on a bed of gravel.

A small water garden partly edged by plants and stones

WATER GARDENS

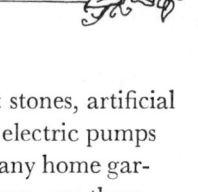

Modern construction materials such as featherweight stones, artificial watersheds, falls and rapids and stream beds, miniature electric pumps and other such devices have made it possible for almost any home gardener to have his own water garden. Few, and far-between, are those gardeners fortunate enough to have a supply of fresh water, such as a stream, on their property and so water for most of these gardens must come from the household service.

The most important consideration is not where the constantly-needed supply of fresh water will come from, but rather, where will it go. Quite often a continuous trickle of water for only a part of the day is enough to meet the needs of the water garden; in this case the outflow can be sent right into the regular drainage system. Perhaps the best solution to the fresh water and drainage problem is in the electric pump—storage tank setup, where the same water can be used over and over again.

This very important matter of water circulation must be settled before any money is invested in a water garden. Where possible, I suggest leaving all the construction work to the experts.

Selecting the Location

The enchantment of a water garden is not actually what can be grown in the cool, inviting water, but rather, what the surface will reflect. Do you want to see the reflection of an ugly old fence, the side of a building, or a pleasant rockery with selected statuary, or well-chosen specimen shrubs when you gaze into your pool? Choose the location wisely.

A good reflection is achieved by constructing the pool so that the water surface is near to the level of the ground. Too often pools are constructed with the water surface several inches lower than the land around it. Where possible, arrange it so that the rapture of the reflection can be caught from the terrace, patio or house.

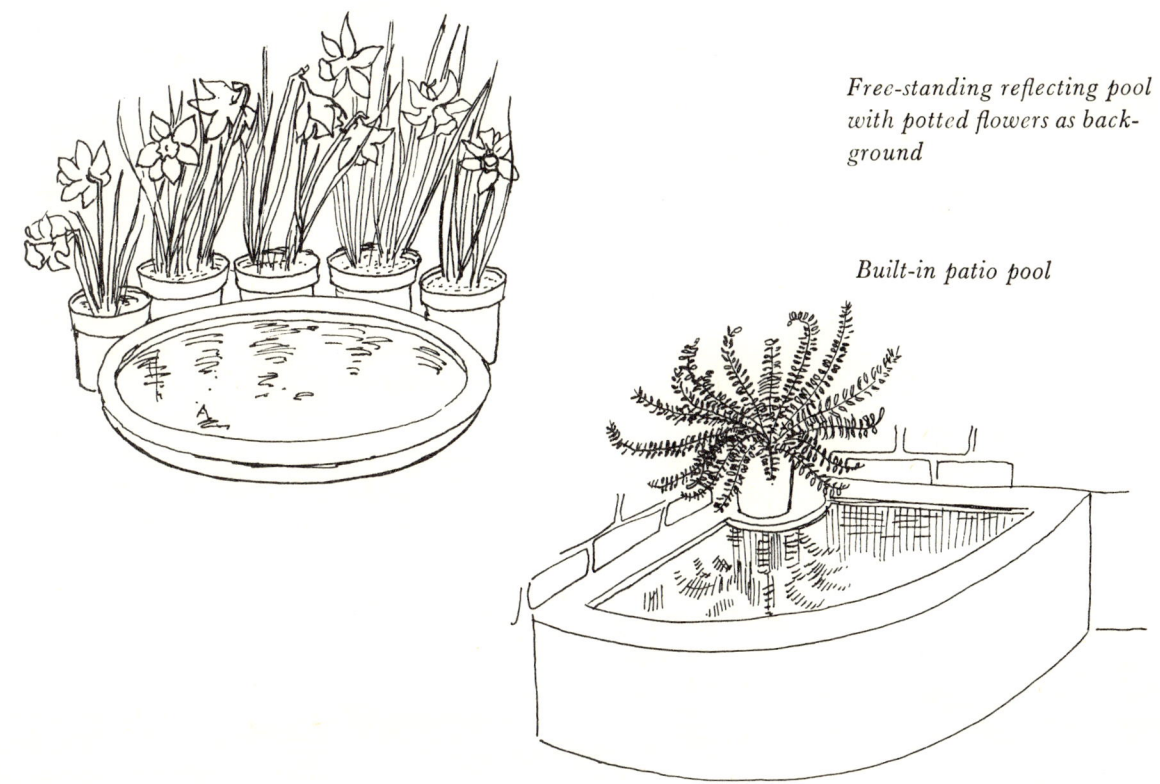

Free-standing reflecting pool with potted flowers as background

Built-in patio pool

Water Garden Plants

Seek out the catalogues and plant lists of suppliers who specialize in water plants. You'll see that there are many plants available which will make your pool garden the highlight of your gardening life. One bonus feature is that the water plants (or pool plants) seldom give you problems and require very little work. Insect pests are almost non-existent with pool plants.

Some water plants, such as the hardy water lilies (and even the tropical water lilies), have their roots in the bottom and grow their leaves on the surface. Some float on the surface, such as duck weed, water hyacinth, and tiny azolla. There are plants that live completely under water—leaves and all—such as arrowhead, elodea, and water hawthorn and others. Right at the shoreline of the pool will grow: the Egyptian paper plant; water poppy; creeping primrose; and water canna. Along poolsides, where water is most apt to seep into the soil, water tolerant plants such as horsetail and elephant ears will thrive.

Remember that this is only a sample of the list of such plants to be found when you order from carefully selected dealers and suppliers. See also those listed under "bog plants".

Cold-zone Water Gardens

Gardeners who live in the "cold zones" cannot expect to launch into pool gardening with the same zeal possible among those who live in milder areas. "Cold zone" people may have to treat all their pool plants as annuals and buy fresh planting stock every spring unless they can give enough protection so that plants will survive the winter and grow afresh every year.

"Cold zone" gardeners have faced this problem with many other areas of their gardening and have often managed to devise a method to bring plenty of their stock through the winters. You can be bold and take a chance even though you live in a really frigid area, but be prepared to accept the winterkill you will likely experience.

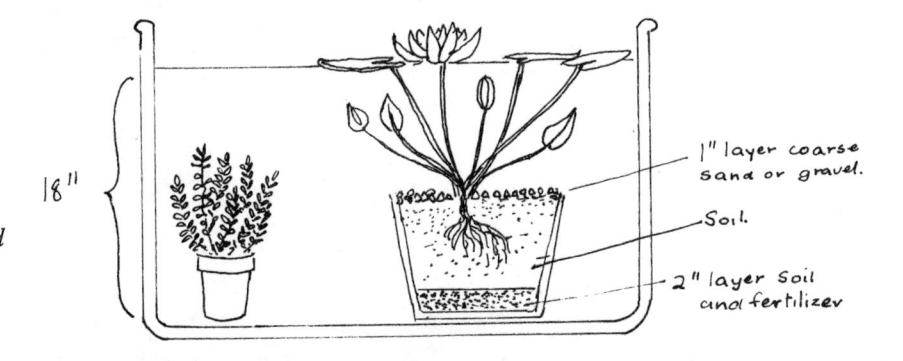

Water plants can be potted and then immersed in a store-bought pool.

Water Lilies

In almost every case, the first pool plant that gardeners buy is a water lily. You may be surprised to know that water lilies come in hundreds of varieties. There are two basic classes—the tropical and the hardy.

When you buy water lilies you will likely be provided with a booklet of cultural instructions. Read those instructions and follow through for best results in growing your water lilies.

In the cold zones, don't expect your tropicals to come through the winter; hardy types likely will survive. Hardy water lilies will die back with the first frost, sleep for the winter under the ice, and revive in the spring.

Water lilies thrive best when they get full sunshine nearly all day long, a fact to remember when you select the location for your pool garden. The pool must be at least two feet deep for lilies.

To prepare the soil, take an old container such as an old tub, wooden box, or dish pan. Fill the container with a mixture with one part dried cow or sheep manure (readily available at your garden centre) and eight parts of good loam. One handful of complete fertilizer should also be added to each bushel of this mixture.

When planting the hardy water lilies, thoroughly wet the soil and press it firmly but gently around the roots of the lily, keeping the tender growing tip above the surface. You are advised not to touch the growing tip as it is extremely delicate. With the lily root held in place by the wet soil, lay a flat stone as a weight over part of it and, without rubbing against the growing parts, cover the whole surface area of the container with crushed stones, or small pebbles, or sand (which will hold the soil mixture in the container when submerged). Submerge the container holding the planted lily to a depth that allows a foot of water to cover the crown of the plant. It might be that some stones will have to be placed under the container to hold it at the proper depth.

The tropical lily varieties are planted in the same manner as described for the hardy lilies, except that the water must be warm, at least 70 degrees, and the lily planted not more than eight inches below the surface. You will need a system in which water is automatically heated in the pumping system. Tropical water lilies come in blue and other colours and also stay open at night, in contrast to the hardy water lilies, which tend to close at the end of the day.

Water lilies often cover a good part of the surface of the pool. Edges can be made exotically beautiful with shallow-rooting water plants. Shelves are often built right into the pool edges to accommodate the edge plants such as wild calla, water chestnut, frog's bit, arrowhead, and water snowflake.

A choice of many water plants is available from the nurseries where water plants are a specialty. Read the planting instructions carefully for advice on their winter care.

TERRACES, PATIOS & DECKS

Gardeners sometimes ask themselves whether the patio or terrace garden or cedar deck is worth the price of construction, or the amount of work required to do the job properly. A well-planned patio or deck, suitably landscaped and planted, will actually be an extension of the living quarters and will allow you to spend many comfortable hours outside. It will also add considerably to the real estate value of the property.

Very often the patio or terrace setting is the focal point of the whole garden and so great care must be taken in the planning stages. An outdoor deck may occupy the entire lounging space available. It can be designed to give the effect of living in a tree-house like Tarzan and Jane, or the effect of a sunken garden slightly below the ground level around you.

A deck is usually just what its name suggests: a flat platform somewhere outside your home where you can sit and breath the fresh air. The decor of the outdoor deck is as varied as the gardener's imagination. When you live squeezed in between other buildings with hardly more than the space of an elevator shaft outdoors, the deck can be built to cover the entire area with all your growing plant life gathered around you in various types of plant containers. Overhead can be hanging baskets, trailing vines and flowering plants, forming an almost solid canopy of growing greenery. Set up a hibachi or small barbecue and you can easily have a secluded rendezvous spot amid otherwise-unpleasant surroundings.

Sometimes the modern building lot is so small that a patio, terrace garden or deck becomes the resident's only solution. These are generally outdoor living areas adjacent to your living quarters.

More often than not, the patio is enclosed by walls constructed in any number of materials and designs to give privacy and intimacy outdoors. An enclosure can be made using a formal hedge, neat dwarf shrubs, trellises or walls of a height suitable to your personal taste. The border around the patio may be simply a selection of suitable plants. The surface of the patio is again a matter of taste: gravel, crushed stone, brick, concrete, asphalt, flag stones, or slabs set in sod.

Plants to Enclose the Terrace or Patio

Often the best choice of planting stock for surrounding the patio or terrace should be slow-growing and small of habit. While the Arctic willow is not considered to be one of the smaller plants, it is a slow-grower and will also add its distinctive foliage texture to the view. Ask

Deck planting can be portable or permanent and can provide shade and beauty.

for Arctic willow (*Salix purpurea* 'Gracilis'). An ideal small and slow-growing flowering shrub is dwarf snowball (*Viburnum opulus* 'Nana'). Two evergreen choices include Korean box (*Buxus microphylla* var. koreana), and Japanese yew (*Taxus cuspidata*). The plant lists will indicate many other suggested plants for this purpose.

The attractiveness of enclosing walls made of shrubs is greatly enhanced on both the inside and outside when further plantings are thoughtfully done. The outside, enclosing shrub wall should be fronted with a selection of low, spreading evergreens with tidy flowering shrubs intermingling to lock the setting together, thus finishing off the picture. These outside-the-hedge plantings almost completely disguise the fact that beyond them lies an open, airy living area, and they also contribute to an extremely attractive view, when seen from other parts of the garden.

From inside the shrub wall the area is very much improved by additional plants set in the immediate foreground. Ground covers may be bearberry (*Arctostaphyllos uva-ursi*), periwinkle (*Vinca minor*), or Japanese spurge (*Pachysandra terminalis*). Go even one step further and among the ground covering plants, mingle such other plants as dwarf iris, Siberian squill, grape hyacinth, snowdrops, crocuses (include some of the autumn-flowering varieties) and, where hardy enough, some of the miniature narcissi. The person sitting on the patio or terrace is treated to a rich, three-tiered layer of growing stock which reveals not a square inch of bare soil along the enclosing hedge.

43

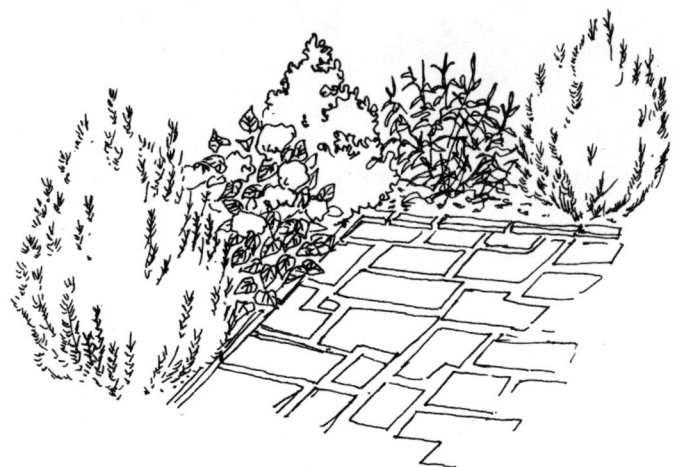

Shrubs make good patio borders.

Points of Accent

When designing the patio and terrace garden, special places for accent plantings, or features, should be allowed. Specimen plants, group plantings, or plant containers (which come in many sizes and descriptions), should be given places of honour in strategic locations.

Some suggested plants, to be included in the master plan of the terrace or patio garden, include the formal dwarf evergreens such as mugho pine, globe cedar, dwarf yew, or the Alberta Spruce (*Picea glauca albertiana* 'Conica'), which are usually planted as individual specimens, or points of accent.

Often a group planting fits the situation better than a specimen. There are any number of small shrubs that suit this purpose such as the daphnes in large variety, Irish junipers, various coloured dogwoods, or some of the hostas, for a few examples.

Design a point of accent in patio floor or walk.

Don't Waste the Nooks, Cracks and Crannies

When terraces and patios are constructed, there are always some tiny places that seem to beg for attention and are often ignored. When care is given to the cracks and crannies the outdoor relaxing area can become truly enchanted. Contrary to popular opinion, there are several plants that can be sown into the cracks between flag stones, patio slabs and other surface materials which will form mats on which a certain amount of traffic can tread without any damage being done. When fragrant herbs, such as lavender and others, are sown or planted between stones and crushed underfoot by traffic they release their fragrance into the air and literally transform the patio or terrace into an exotic oasis on a warm summer's night. Other mat-forming crevice plants include *Thymus serphyllum* and its variety of cultivars (another herb), and *Sagina repens, Phlox subulata, Arenaria verna,* and *Veronica repens*. These perennial plants will usually thrive in tiny places forming colourful and fragrant mats year after year.

There are also annual plants that will take over a crack on a terrace or patio floor and provide colour all summer when sown right into the places where they are to grow. Some of these include: single and double portulaca and the compact form of sweet alysum. Where conditions are hot and sunny, the annual ice plant may also be sown (look for *Mesembryanthemum*).

The patio will stay dry when potted plants are allowed to stand on small bed of gravel or marble chips.

Raised beds keep roots moist and undisturbed.

Plant Your Own Spring View

Often the view seen from the patio or terrace is as important in early spring as at all other seasons. Sometimes while parts of the garden are displaying dismal-looking brown mud, other parts are still covered with snow and the general outlook is one of dismay as the viewer fears spring will never arrive. Very-early flowering shrubs, strategically located to be seen from the house and patio or the terrace, soon bring a welcome relief from the drabness of late winter and early spring. Snow may lie in one section of the garden while white, waxy flowers are blooming on the white mezereon (*Daphne mezereum* 'Album') in another section, hopefully where it can be seen to best advantage. Other early flowering shrubs include: dwarf Anthony Waterer spirea (*Spiraea bumalda* 'Anthony Waterer'), Korean golden bells (*Forsythia ovata*), and Lemoine's deutzia (*Deutzia lemoinei*).

Pots of flowers are plunged to the rim in soil. Soil is covered with gravel or marble chips, as a decorative mulch. This is good summertime use of some house plants.

Tubs and Containers

Plant containers on the deck, patio, and terrace have probably done more to bring the modern northern garden into the Seventies than anything else. Tubs and containers have made it possible to update gardening habits so that it is now possible to enjoy the colours and foliage textures of plants that have always been considered tabu in northern conditions. We have become a people who move outdoors on the first warm days of spring and stay there through until the leaves change colour in the fall.

The backyard, balcony, deck, patio, or terrace of today has been transformed into an area of luxury. Pools, sun decks, hibachis, barbecues, fountains, statuary, waterfalls, have all been enhanced by truly portable gardens consisting of exotic and dazzling summer flowers. Plant containers, on wheels and otherwise, now bring the garden to the gardener with complete portability. Now it is possible for containers of living flowers to be arranged up-close and in-tight to surround intimate outdoor gatherings, and, at other times, moved further back to become colourful accent points.

Choosing what to grow in your plant containers is entirely a matter of individual taste. If you prefer the kind of beauty, colour and fragrance that come from the hundreds of varieties of the commonly-known annuals and perennials, you will have a display of traditional beauty. In situations where more exotic conversation-causing flowers are desired, then a little thoughtful consideration about what to buy is required. Some container plant suggestions follow.

Tender plants such as English holly, bay laurel, or blue hydrangeas thrive in tubs but (except in the mild areas of the west), they must be brought indoors for the winter and kept almost dry in their containers. Take them back outdoors after frost in the spring.

Blue-Lily-of-the-Nile, or African lily, (*Agapanthus*) is a tuberous-rooted plant which produces beautiful flowers. It can be planted in a patio tub or plant container and left outdoors all summer long. Before frost in the fall the container must be wheeled indoors, leaving the plant in the soil intact for the winter.

The yellow-orange South American *Cypella herbertii* is a beautiful, rare plant that produces flowers all through the summer. Dig the bulbs out of the soil in the fall and store at 45 to 50 degrees for the winter. The plant which is thought to be the biblical Lily-of-the-field (*Anemone coronaria*) provides a glorious mixture of colours. The bulbs should be dug up and stored indoors for the winter.

A very rare and exotic patio container plant is the fabulous Japanese egret flower (*Habenaria radiata*). It is a terrestial orchid which needs to be grown in the shade in small, four to six inch patio containers. Store indoors before frost.

Other sub-tropical and exotic plants to grow and flow in portable patio plant containers (or tubs) include: the Pineapple lily (*Eucomis*); Gloriosa lily; the very fragrant sea daffodils of Peru in many different varieties and colours; the montbretias which produce a gladiolus-like flower that can be brought indoors after the first frost to continue blooming; the bulbous ranunculus (*Ranunculus asiaticus*), also called the turban ranunculus, which has flowers in the shape of small turbans.

With the advent of the sliding glass door and plate glass window, which often extends from floor to ceiling, the portable plant containers can now be brought right into the living room for their winter display. The possibilities are many and varied for patio, deck, and terrace plant containers. Imagine a patio container filled with amaryllis in the living room in December? Utterly fabulous!

Ornamental shrubs can be wheeled from place to place.

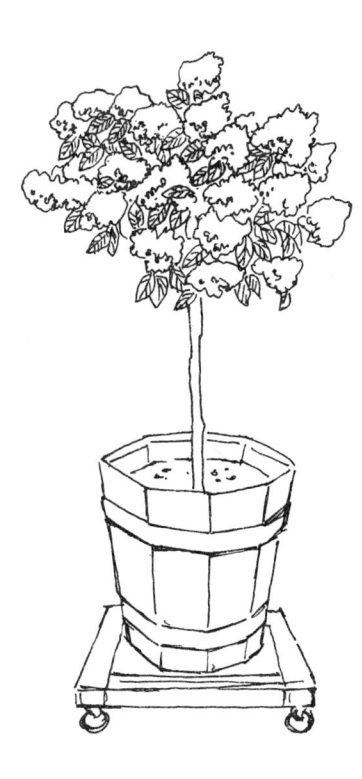

Entranceways inside and out are natural places for living plants.

THE FRAGRANT GARDEN

One of the rewards the gardener can look forward to as payment for all the work, time, loving care, worrying, and money invested in the garden is a peaceful hour or two on a summer's evening. That period of the day as the sun makes its transition from full daylight to dusk is when the chosen plants of the garden radiate a bonus feature—their fragrance. The redolent perfume plus the mystic colour brilliances of twilight contributes a certain romantic, restful atmosphere that nothing else on earth can provide. Don't miss out on this glorious aspect of your garden. Be sure to include several of the fragrant flowers and plants when planning whether in a formal bed, informal arrangement, patio planter, balcony box, terrace garden or shrub hedge. A minimum amount of sunlight will be acceptable.

The flowering annuals are the quickest fragrant flowers to establish in the garden as they can be sown where they are to flower and later thinned to a spacing of about two or three inches apart. It is a fact of nature that flowers of white and yellow radiate the most delightful fragrance; these also appear at their colourful best in the evening.

You have been missing out on one of the better things in life if you have not enjoyed the evening fragrances of the delightful night-scented stock, which exudes perfume in profusion at twilight. Sow its seeds in early May for summer-long bloom and fragrance. It grows eighteen inches high and produces rather tiny flowers.

A good garden partner for night-scented stock is the moonflower. Normally the moonflower is grown as a climber on trellises or walls, or other support, where it performs very well. In this case, train the moonflower (*Calonyction aculeatum*) to grow in mounds on small twigs a few inches off the ground. The moonflower only opens its flowers to the coolness of evening when its scent is sweetest.

One of the most familiar of the fragrant garden plants is flowering tobacco, or Nicotiana. During the daylight hours the flowers remain closed and the plant is rather inconspicuous, even though it grows up to thirty-six inches high, but in the evening the flowers open and the fragrance literally fills the garden. There are now several varieties of Nicotiana, some in varying colours, others of different sizes.

The white and yellow varieties of petunias seem to gradually increase their fragrance as the evening turns into night.

The little, spreading plant sweet alyssum (*Lobularia maritima*), which is usually planted as a front edger, or space filler, is now also considered to be a good fragrance plant. Experimenters and plant breeders have developed several new varieties which are pleasantly fragrant, a fact which should be kept in mind when asking for sweet alyssum next time.

Another extremely fragrant annual plant which actually takes its name from its evening perfuming habits, is the evening primrose *Oenothera odorata*. Most of the evening primroses are hardy perennials which bear yellow flowers that open in the evening. The three-foot tall true evening-scented primrose (*Oenothera lamarckiana*) is the most common of the perennial varieties.

Perfume in the Patio Planters

Although it is a perennial plant that thrives in the tropics, we can grow the angel's trumpets (*Datura*) as though they were annuals, in patio pots and containers. From mid-summer to September (first frost) these plants produce their huge trumpet-shaped flowers in colours of white, mauve, or yellow. There are several different varieties available, the most fragrant is *Datura metel*.

Plan for Fragrance in the Shrubbery too

While it may be novel and unique to possess containers and points of accent which are of brilliant and even fragrant flowers, perennials and bulbs, still, many gardeners prefer the old-fashioned gracefulness and charm of bushes and shrubs that have a sweet scent as well as sometimes attractive flowers and foliage, or berries. There are many kinds of shrubs that can be planted as fragrant points of beauty, and, of course, they do not have to be moved from one season to another—they stay where you put them all year round.

Let's first consider the fragrant shrubs for gardeners on the west coast who are blessed with the mildest growing conditions. The adventurous green-thumber in other parts of the country might try some of these tender shrubs if he or she can provide a very well-sheltered place in which to grow them, but be prepared for disappointment. One such shrub to be tried in a protected area is the common woodbine. Provide half-shade and train it to creep along the ground under the protection of other, hardier shrubs. Common woodbine is perhaps more widely known as climbing English honeysuckle (*Lonicera periclymenum*). This shrub has a almost too-heavy, sweet scent. Another, is the large-flowered *Viburnum carlcephalum*.

Westerners along the coast can also count on success with such fragrant shrubs as mountain pieris, the lily of the valley shrub, (*Pieris floribunda*), sweet jasmine (*Jasminum officinalis*) with its clove-like fragrance, Mexican orange (*Choisya ternata*), rosemary (*Rosemarinus officinalis*), Korean Spice viburnum (*Viburnum carlesi*), Judd's viburnum (*Viburnum juddii*), and, the newest of the snowballs, the amazing hybrid viburnum (*Viburnum carlcephalum*).

Elsewhere across the land a vast selection of fragrant shrubs will thrive and require very little care. A careful search of the plant listings will indicate a large number from which to choose. Some of the most common fragrant, hardy shrubs are listed below.

The shrub that is probably the most fragrant and yet the least known is the Carolina allspice (*Calycanthus floridus*). This shrub features fine-textured leaves which bring a touch of beauty, and when crushed slightly, transmit a delicate fragrance. Placing the Carolina allspice near entranceways so that traffic will brush against the foliage often brings the fragrance indoors with the guests.

Such dwarf shrubs as the Daphnes bring their fragrance to the home setting very early in the season. The early flowering Mezereon (*Daphne mezereum*) is a good selection, as is Burkwood Daphnes (*Daphne burkwoodii*) with its glossy, evergreen leaves and pink-to-white, tube-shaped flowers.

Fragrance in late spring is assured by a planting of common mock orange (*Philadelphus coronaris*). This shrub can either be allowed to grow naturally in its own arching shape with abundant flowers and pleasing foliage colours, or can be shaped by shearing and clipping. There are many varieties of mock orange available.

Where there's space under a window for French hybrid lilacs, a great deal of this familiar and pleasant fragrance will waft indoors and fill the home with the essence of spring itself. Another fragrant lilac is the Chinese lilac (*Syringa chinensis*). Its perfume can be enjoyed to the fullest when the shrub is planted against a wall.

Roses are fragrant, decorative, trainable and can be grown in confined spaces.

The viburnums, also called the snowball bushes, are not only fragrant but also produce a handsome show of bloom in the spring; some also produce long-lasting berries. There are many selections of viburnum. No fragrant garden would be complete without a few of the countless available varieties of roses.

Fragrance in a Garden Three Feet Square

Sometimes the gardener is faced with a space so small that the first impulse is to pave it over and forget it altogether. However, a space about three feet square may be the only place available for gardening or anything else and even with one so small there is no need to let it go to waste. Bring some colour, beauty and fragrance to this tiniest of gardens by planting a climbing rose. One suggested variety is the Sympathie climbing rose which features double-red flowers resembling the glorious hybrid tea rose flowers. Give the plant something to climb on, such as an old-fashioned hitching post, or an imitation lamp standard, or possibly even a working gas lamp. Three feet square is plenty of room for this project so long as at least a few hours of sunlight play on the climber each day. There is an almost endless list of climbers including the newest everblooming varieties available and suitable for such pillar-planting purposes.

Roses come in various forms, standard, climbing, bush, and can be used in many ways.

The Sweetest of Trees

The sweet smell of success is perhaps its most flamboyant in the fragrant trees. Some suggested fragrant trees include: the oleaster, or Russian olive (*Elaeagnus angustifolia*), which grows to about thirty-five feet with silvery green leaves; and most fragrant of the crabapple trees, Bechtel's crab tree, which produces extremely fragrant flowers that are often two to two-and-a-half inches across with a strong, rose-like scent. Of the large size trees, the little leaf linden is most fragrant when in bloom. Check the plant lists for the names of others.

FLORAL PAVING

By borrowing a custom of Europe and England, we can enjoy the charm of floral paving, a "flat rock garden", which is mostly stone and a few well-chosen plants. The plants are those with a creeping or tufting habit. How much more attractive is a path of floral paving than the more usual poured concrete!

In tiny or awkward places, instead of laying two or three sods in a space which would be difficult to mow, lay stones instead. As long as it will not be used as running space for children, you can treat all or part of a small garden in this way.

Floral paving is different from the seeding of cracks and crevices mentioned elsewhere in that the soil beneath the stones must be well-prepared before the stones are laid. As a minimum, a layer of three inches of well-prepared soil should make up the substratum, consisting of a mixture of equal parts sand, peat moss and good garden soil.

It would be folly to expect any plants between the stones to stand up to constant, heavy traffic without soon being ground to oblivion, and so a few things should be considered when laying the stones. The largest

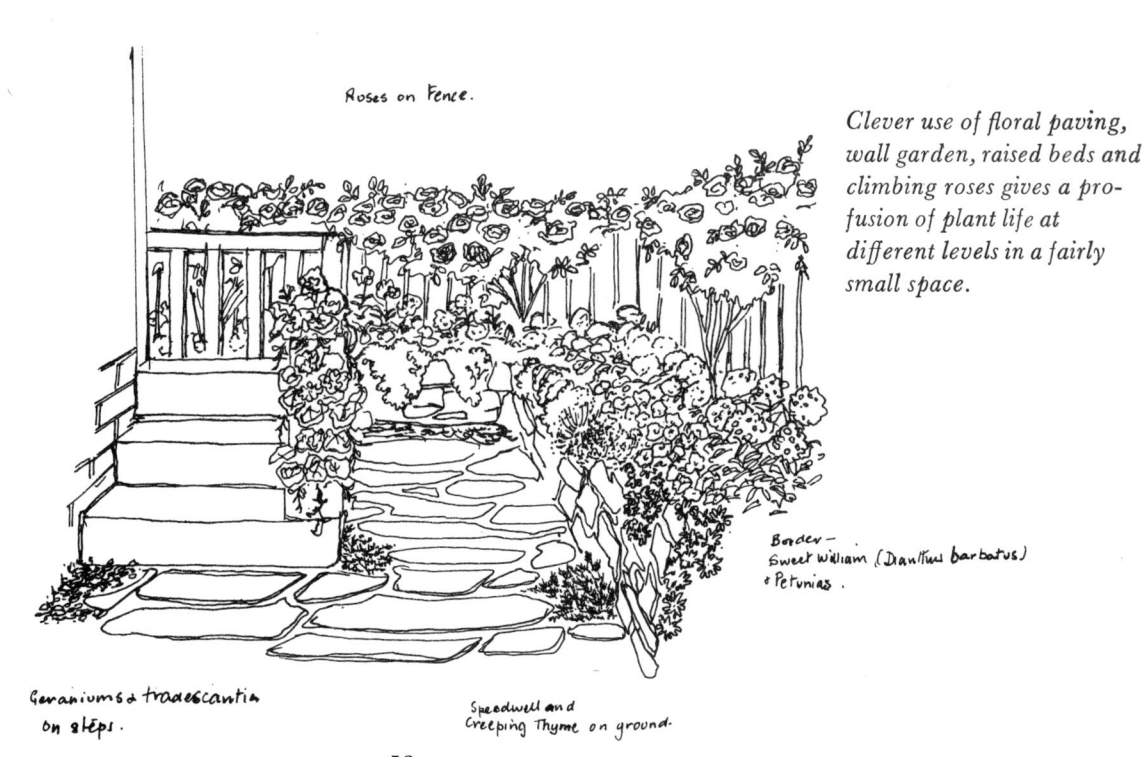

Clever use of floral paving, wall garden, raised beds and climbing roses gives a profusion of plant life at different levels in a fairly small space.

stones should be laid where traffic will be heaviest, smaller stones at corners, edges and away from the most used places. Places the plants in areas where the *least* traffic will tread on them.

As each stone is set into place on top of the prepared three inches of soil, it should be thoroughly tested to make certain that it is solidly firm. A space of about one inch between large stones is acceptable, although wider spaces are quite in order as all mistakes are soon covered with plant life.

Much easier planting is guaranteed when the plants are ready to be put in place as the stones are being laid. You will probably be pleasantly surprised to see how quickly the paving plants establish themselves.

Selecting the Floral Paving Plants

Some of the plants suitable for paving plantings may be available only as seeds and should be started in pots prior to planting out. Remember that plants such as the small herbs can be sown in pots in May and transplanted the following spring, or possibly in the fall of the same year. Apply water to these pots of seeds no less than twice a week. Have patience; some of these seeds may require a full season of frost (winter) before germinating. You may have to wait two years before finally getting transplants large enough to place between the rocks.

The following lists are by no means the only plants that can be used in pathway planting. Half the fun is in searching and keeping an eye open for various species. Watch the seed and plant lists for the spreading, tufting, carpeting or matting varieties of plants.

The Tufting Plants

Among the selection of tufting plants you will find *Artemisia* 'Silver Mound', and the little bluets (*Houstonia caerulea*) with many blue and white flowers. The tufting thrift (*Armeria caespitosa*) has grass-like leaves and double pink everlasting flowers.

The Carpeting Plants

Among the lists of carpeting, or matting plants are the various forms of the common herb thyme (*Thymus serpyllum*). Moss pinks or ground phlox (*Phlox subulata*) will thrive almost anywhere and come in a variety of colours.

A good matting plant with blue flowers is creeping speedwell (*Veronica filiformis*) which also features a foliage that is sometimes almost evergreen in habit.

White matting flowers are available in the white snow-in-summer (*Cerastium tomentosum*). Yellow flowers are the feature of creeping draba (*Draba repens*) and double bird's foot trefoil (*Lotus corniculatus flora plena*), and the yellow alyssum, or Basket of Gold (*Alyssum saxatile*).

General Care

Weeds must be controlled before they are allowed to gain a foothold in the crevices from which they are almost impossible to remove once established. Use extremely careful application of weedkiller applied *to the weed only*; it should be remembered that these chemicals will kill everything they touch.

Rampant plants may have to be cut back to be kept in control. The parts removed can often be replanted in other places where growth is scarce.

No winter protection of the plants is necessary if the plants selected are known to be hardy in your district; otherwise, appropriate steps must be taken to see them through the cold weather. Try to educate all the family that these flat-rockery plants should not be stepped on in frosty weather, or when snow is on the ground, as they are easily destroyed at these times.

APARTMENT GARDENS

The apartment dweller gets the opportunity to use his imagination, and to take advantage of all the new kinds of equipment and plant containers perhaps more so than other gardeners. A challenge, the apartment garden can be, with work, just as beautiful and as productive as one maintained at ground level. The apartment gardener is by no means confined to conventional house plants, but can grow a wide variety of garden plants, flowers, and even vegetables.

On a balcony, with the help of window boxes and other plant containers, there is a wide choice of possible garden types. Where there is no balcony, the window sill garden and hanging baskets will provide space. Later in this book, a section is devoted to gardening under lights, which may well be the apartment's only garden area.

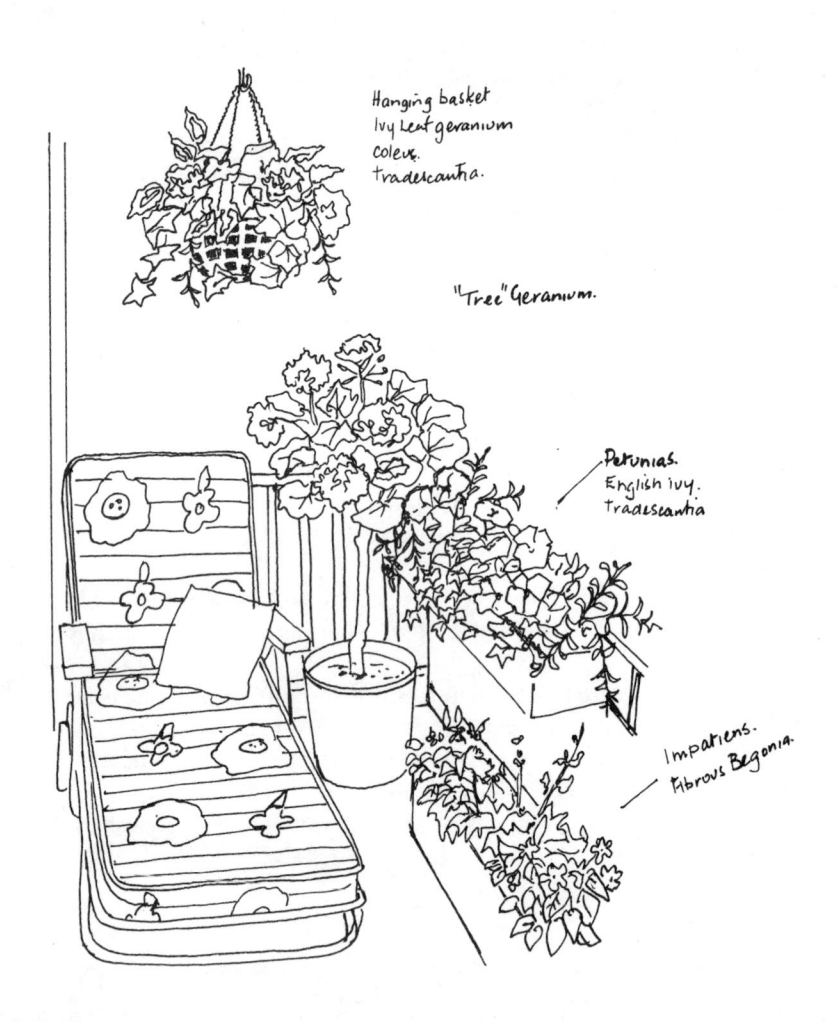

A balcony garden makes good use of various containers.

Watering

When watering plant containers, the entire amount of soil must be thoroughly wet. Never be satisfied that enough water has been applied until you are certain that the soil is wet from top to bottom. Waiting and watching for water to drip out the bottom of the container is not a good enough indicator that the soil is wet enough to do the right job. Very often water will find an easy course through a vein of sand or some other non-organic material and simply run straight to the bottom and out the drainage holes leaving all but a small area totally dry. Having a well-mixed and balanced supply of organic matter in the soil will assure that enough water will be retained. Before applying water again, test the soil to see that it is dry to the touch, then water thoroughly.

Dribbling water down the sides of a container does not water the whole rootball. This will cause shrinkage and the soil and roots will shrivel causing unwanted air space on all sides.

Take a sharp stick and loosen soil so that water will permeate all through root ball. If small enough the container may be plunged in water until saturated.

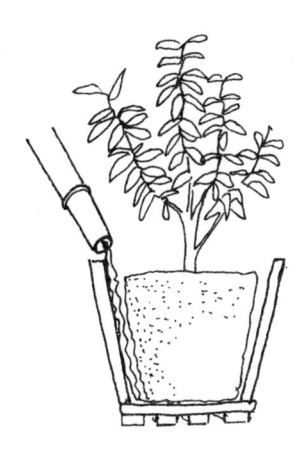

One type of plant container, designed especially for apartment balconies and other such locations, is built with a metal tray placed under a false, wooden bottom from which several wicks extend up into the soil. As long as the metal tray is kept constantly filled with water, by topping up every day or so, the soil always contains just the right degree of moisture. It may pay you to shop for such a container so that your watering worries can be minimized.

The one fact that should never be forgotten when caring for plant life that grows in a container of any kind, whether a window box, patio planter, hanging basket or flower pot, is that it must be watered faithfully. In almost every case the roots of plants in containers are never more than a few inches away from the dry atmosphere on all sides. Dry surrounding air dries the soil which in turn dries the roots, an effect not tolerated by most plants. Extremely dry roots become detrimental to the plant; continuously drenching soil is bad, too. The rule is: never too dry and never too wet.

Depending on the location of the container and the structure of the soil within it, the necessity of daily watering is quite possible. In some cases you may need to apply water only once or twice each week. In constant sunshine, or in a steady breeze, the soil in a container may dry out in a few hours. Placed in a shady spot offering protection from prevailing winds the soil may remain moist for several days.

Feeding

It should be remembered that soil in containers cannot draw on mother earth for continued plant nourishment. The vital minerals and trace elements that plants require to survive must be supplied by the gardener. An application of a balanced plant food once each month would not be wasted. Fertilizers are now available in many different forms—dry powder, crystals, pills, water soluables, and liquids—any of which can be easily applied.

Sprinkle the dry fertilizers on the surface of the soil and gently work them in without damaging the tender, shallow roots. If dry fertilizer is spilled on foliage remove it immediately by gently shaking or brushing the leaves or they may burn. Dry fertilizers must be watered well into the soil after application. Liquid fertilizers can be applied directly to the soil and onto the foliage of the plants without fear of burning. The hairy leaves of such plants as African violets and gloxinias should never be touched with liquid of any kind, including liquid fertilizers.

Remember the Dangers of Frost

The balcony garden is extremely vulnerable to frost simply because you, the gardener, cannot see the frost signals felt and seen all around at ground level. Watch the weather forecasts and whenever there is a danger of frost in your neighbourhood, bring in those hanging baskets for the night and cover the balcony planters and window boxes with weighted newspaper or other insulating material.

Soil for the Containers

Great strides forward have taken place in the development of planting mediums so that it is now possible for the apartment resident to cultivate a garden without using a single grain of true soil. Plant developers at Cornell University, for example, have created a planting medium that is so highly recommended, that those who use it are cautioned that they will likely have to cut and snip continuously to keep their super-vigorous plants in check. The Cornell University people gave their new planting medium the name of "peatlite", probably because it is made up of equal parts of peat moss and vermiculite. This new product is very light-weight and is weed and disease-free. The town or city gardener who cannot buy "peatlite" locally could make up a batch of his own.

The following recipe, prepared in the quantity stated below (or in smaller amounts, as required), will provide two bushels of peatlite (half the amounts will make up one bushel, etc.):

one bushel of number 2, 3, or 4, horticultural vermiculite;
one bushel of Canadian or German sphagnum peat moss;
ten level teaspoonsful of ground limestone;
five level teaspoonsful of potassium nitrate;
one level teaspoonful of chelated iron;
gradually add one gallon of warm water.

Where the gardener does not have enough room in his plant containers to hold this amount of homemade peatlite, surplus stock can be stored in a plastic bag. It keeps for up to six months. For a place to mix such things in the apartment, you could use a plastic garbage pail, or a sturdy cardboard box lined with a couple of plastic garbage bags (one inside the other for extra strength). For tiny amounts, prepare this sterilized mixture on a covered table top.

As a growing mixture, peatlite requires a regular and continuing fertilizer program with applications of water soluble fertilizers according to the maker's directions, usually added with alternate waterings. The peatlite mix can also be effectively used as a starting medium for seeds.

Instead of peatlite, a general mixture of equal parts of garden soil, peat moss, and sand will do the job. You may want to add some perlite (an inorganic soil conditioner), or vermiculite, or maybe additional soil and composted cow or sheep manure, which is now available odorless.

You can buy the soil in plastic bags thus eliminating all the fuss and bother of mixing your own. Check the label to make certain that the soil you buy is fully sterilized and also weed-free. In almost every case these bagged soils are a balanced mixture of soil, organic material, plant food, and just the right amounts of sand and humus, and thus ideal for the apartment gardener.

Selecting the Planter

It is sometimes a perplexing matter to choose the balcony planter. It will be helpful to know that no matter what length the railing or balcony wall is where the planters will be attached, planters each three feet long are ideal. When they are longer than this they may be difficult to handle and structurally weak.

Whether or not the boxes are custom-built for the specific balcony or window sill, they may be painted only on the outside (never on the inside) with any good housepaint, or stained and varnished with products that do not contain creosote, as this chemical is known to be harmful to plants. No matter what style, length, weight, or material used, planters and boxes must be securely fastened in place to prevent accidents.

Planters come in all shapes and sizes.

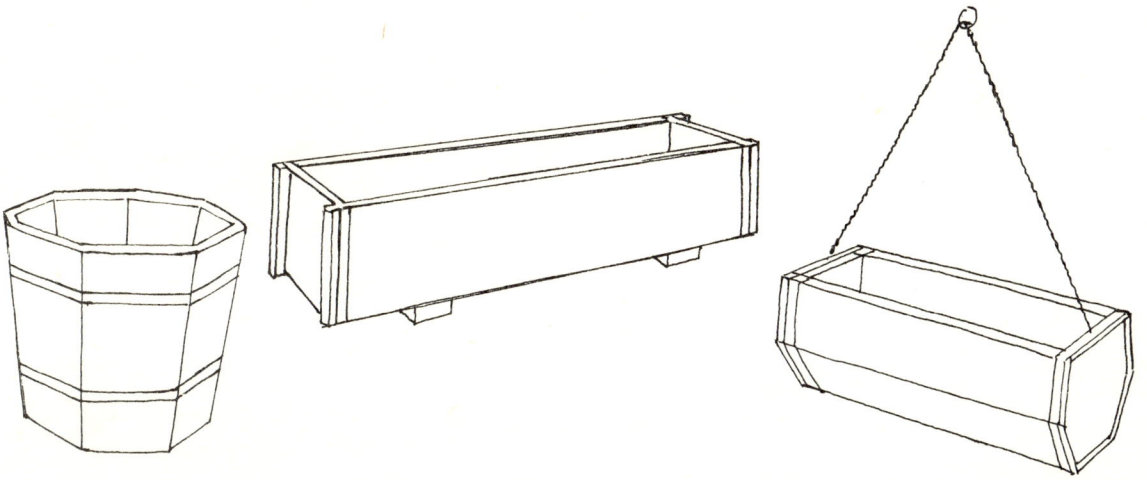

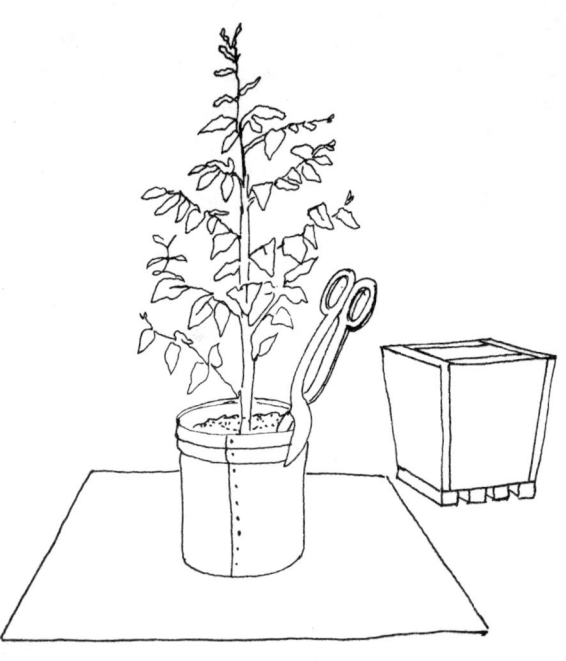

From nursery container to planting tub.

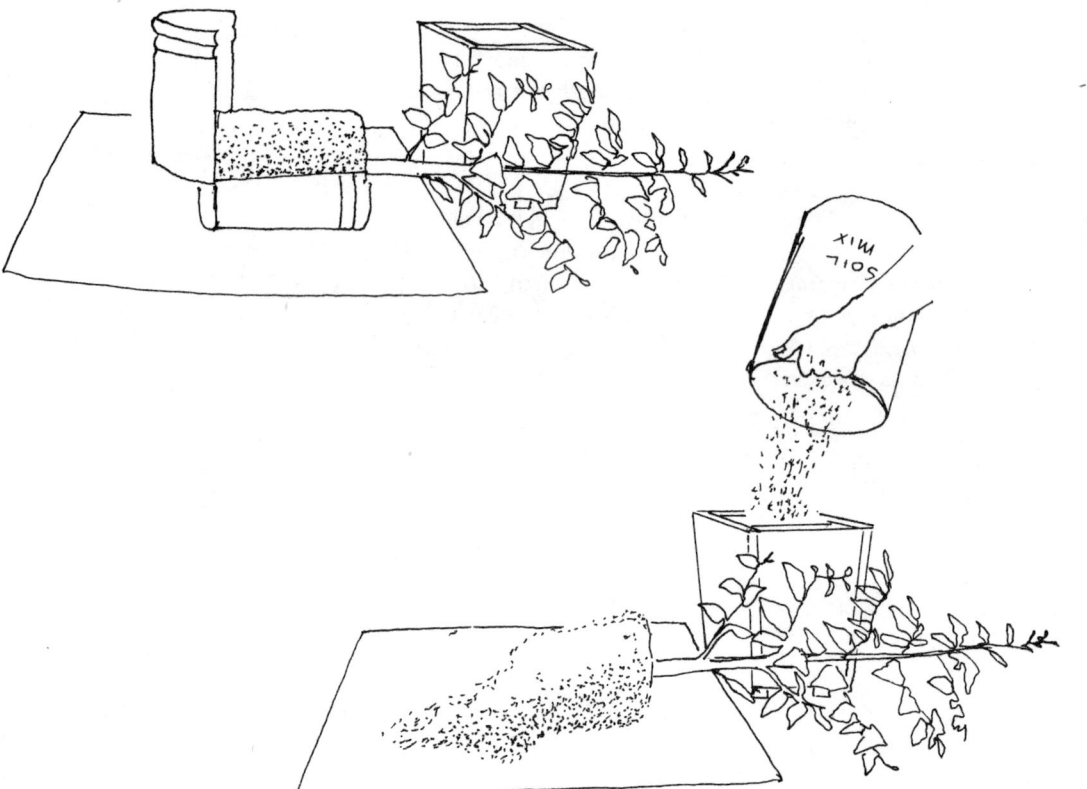

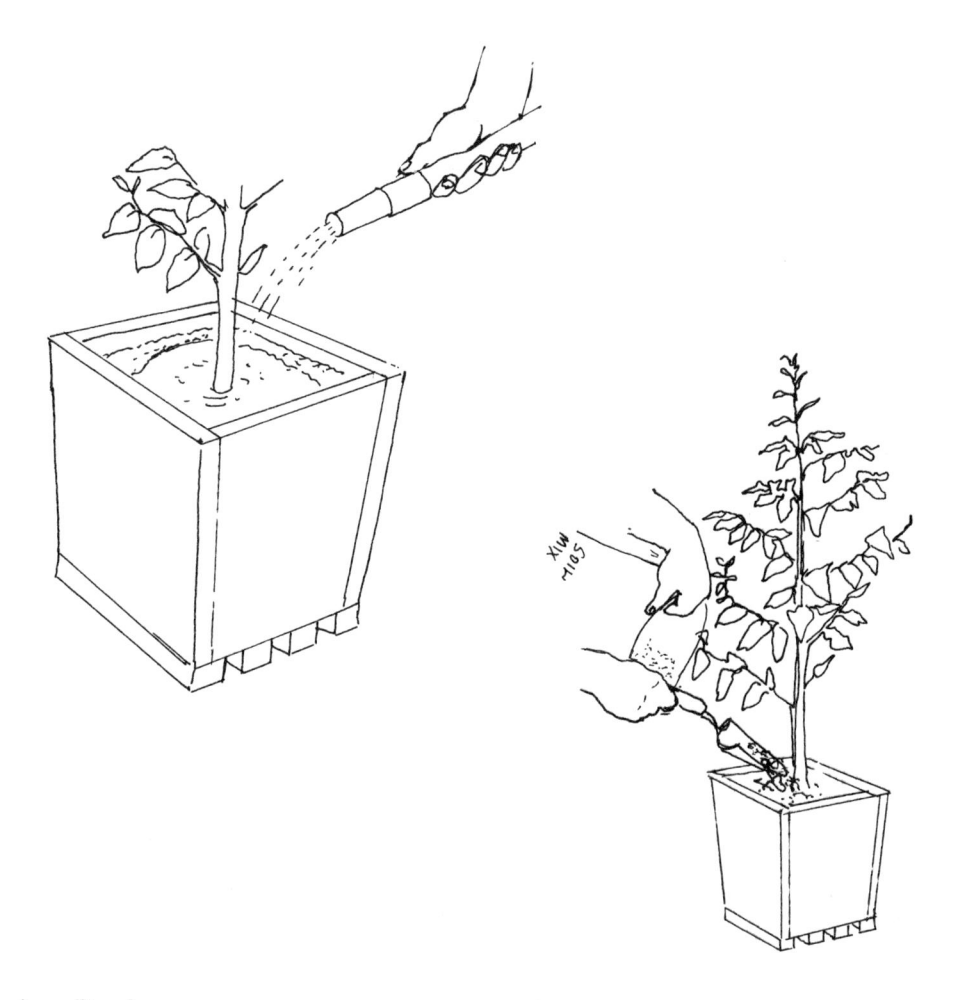

Hanging Baskets

In cases where the building designer left absolutely no place to put either balcony planters or railing hangers, or even windowsill boxes, the next choice is the hanging basket. These may be also used in conjunction with other planters as well as by themselves.

So vast and varied is the selection of hanging baskets, ranging all the way from wire, and wicker, to molded plastics, the choice is almost endless. Whatever means or device is used to hang the baskets, make sure that they will be held *securely* in place.

It should be remembered that when the baskets must hang in the shade of a roof overhang or the balcony on the floor above, only shade-tolerant plants should be used. All plants in containers are vulnerable to fast moisture loss and so their watering needs must be tended to regularly.

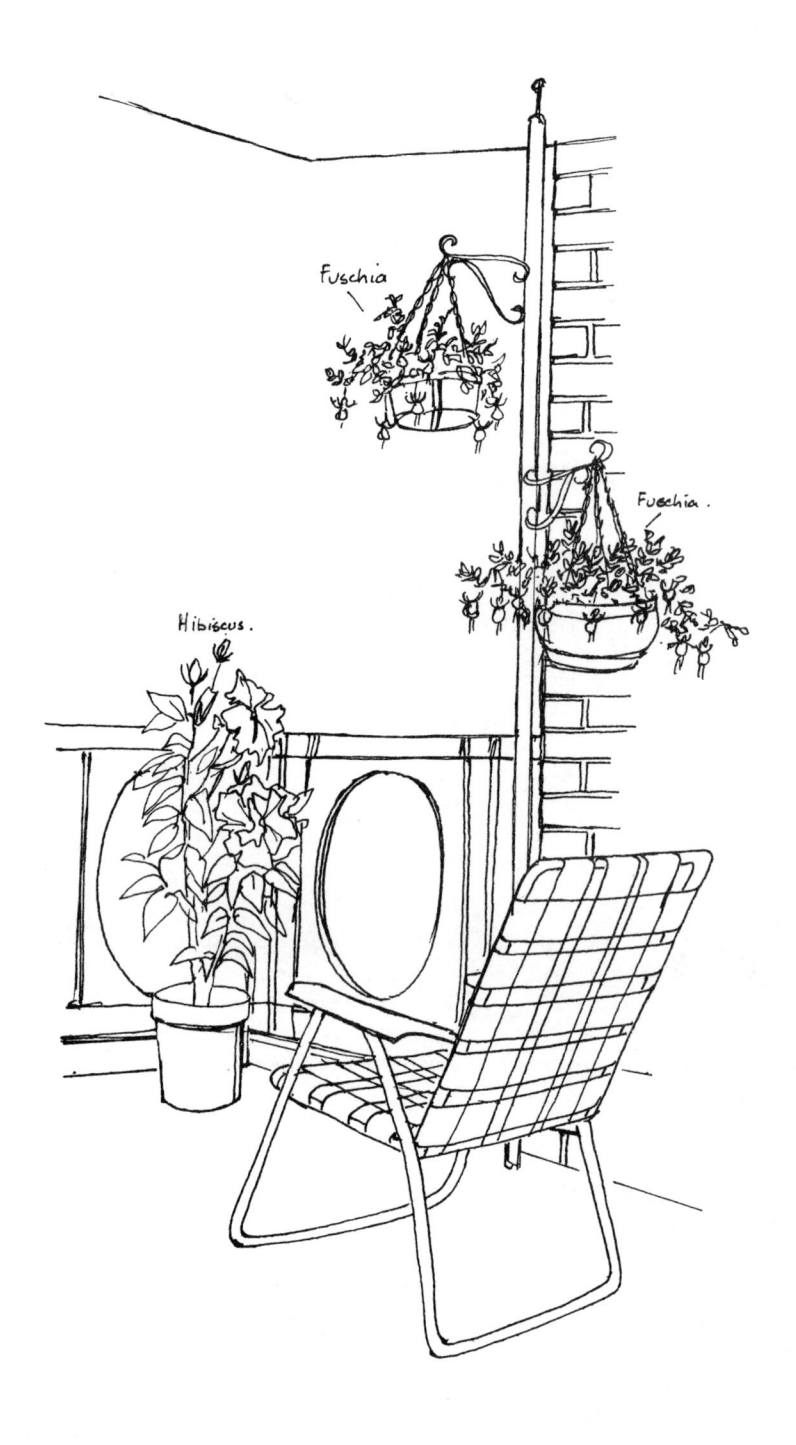

Baskets of flowers trail from pole on an apartment balcony. The sturdy spring-loaded pole can be used indoors in the winter.

One recommended planting procedure for hanging baskets is as follows: Line each basket with a fibrous material, such as a sheet of compressed peat moss, or perhaps one or two layers of clean burlap, then fill it with a planting medium containing plenty of moisture-retaining material, such as peatlite. Knock the plants out of their containers and firm the rootball with its soil attached into the medium in the basket.

One of the special advantages of the hanging baskets, with their pendulous, cascading plants and flowers, is that they can be as portable as the gardener desires. For example: flowers naturally grow towards the light, usually facing out from the balcony or window. When you want, the baskets can be turned to have glorious masses of flowers facing inward towards you and your guests. Baskets can also be taken down once or twice a week and sat in a bucket or tub of water and allowed to soak up all the water they need. While the flowers in the baskets are enjoying their twice weekly drenching, they can also be given a shower from above and then a quick once-over to remove old, faded, and dead flower heads and leaves, and straggly growth.

Steps in planting a hanging basket.
Line basket with fibrous material.
Fill with suitable soil.
Place plants in hanging basket.

Plants that Hang and Trail

The following list of plants contains only a few suggestions for which plants to grow in the apartment garden. A study of catalogues and plant lists will uncover the names of many others.

The first category that most apartment dwellers look for is the hanging and trailing type. The new types of so-called weeping carnations with the habit of drooping over the side of a container make an ideal trailing balcony plant. Some of the most recommended hanging and trailing plants are the following:

Cascading petunia
Cup and Saucer
English Ivy (Shade tolerant)
Geranium, ivy-leaved varieties
German Ivy (Shade tolerant)
Fuschia (Shade tolerant)
Lantana (Shade tolerant)
Lobelia (Shade tolerant)
Morning Glory
Sweet Alyssum
Trailing begonia (Shade tolerant)
Thunbergia
Wandering Jew (Shade tolerant)

A metal or plastic saucer suspended under hanging basket to catch drips

The low-growing clumps of flowers
　Ageratum
　Dwarf Marigold
　Fibrous Begonia (Shade tolerant)
　Lobelia (Shade tolerant)
　Nierembergia
　Pansy (Shade tolerant)
　Portulaca
　Sweet Alyssum
　Torenia (Shade tolerant)

The plants that stand upright and erect
　Balsam
　Browallia (Shade tolerant)
　Cornflower
　Dianthus
　Dwarf Nicotiana (Shade tolerant)
　Dwarf Snapdragon
　Fuschia (Shade tolerant)
　Geranium
　Marigold
　Mignonette
　Impatiens (Shade tolerant)

Upward growing vines
　Canary Vine
　Cup-and-Saucer vine
　Morning Glory
　Nasturtium
　Scarlet-Runner Bean
　Thunbergia

Hanging baskets containing trailing or pendulous plants can be plunged into a basin that stands on an upturned flower pot to protect the tips of stems.

Bowl of water

House Plants on the Balcony

Many an apartment-dweller plant-enthusiast keeps pots and containers of many kinds of house plants all year round. Be cautioned that you should not recklessly place these indoor house plants out onto an exposed balcony, or hanging basket, or railing hanger, or window box. Always keep the growing habits of those plants in mind. Your shade-loving African violets should never be placed in the sunlight. Foliage plants that have always been kept in a subdued light will suffer a real set-back if suddenly placed in the sun. Indoor ferns would surely perish in the chilly breeze and bright light of an unprotected outdoor location. On the other hand, your indoor geraniums will thrive in the fullest, brightest sunlight a balcony or windowsill can offer—as long as they are kept moist and fed.

Very few "outdoor" plants can survive indoors. You may be lucky with marigolds, snapdragons, and certain other container grown annuals but they do not make good indoor house plants. Remember when you are selecting your plants that they are for locations either inside or outside, but seldom do the two mix successfully.

The Standards

The class of plants often called standards include shrubs and trees that are grown in tubs, or other containers where they spend their entire growing life. These include roses, fuschias, cherry trees, etc. This class of plant can be brought indoors from the balcony during the frigid weather to be protected from the severe ravages of winter. In some towns and cities there are greenhouses whose operators will store tub-held "standards" for a nominal fee, sometimes picking them up and delivering them back again in the spring.

Growing Plants Need Not Be Expensive

Many gardening opportunities are available for those who fall into the general classification of "apartment gardener" that can be accomplished for pennies, or no-cost at all. The town or city gardener who is forced to pave dingy little back alley areas with flag stones, or round slabs, or to otherwise change the scene structurally, cannot do so without spending some money.

However, if all you want to do is see some green, the next time you peel carrots or parsnips, save the top half-inch at the leafy end and set them in a saucer of water on a windowsill. Keep the water level at about a quarter to half an inch, and you will be surprised at how quickly the tops will regrow.

Basic house plant shapes

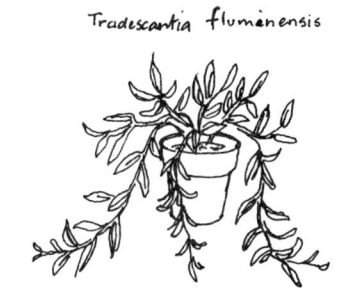

Tradescantia fluminensis

Trailing or pendulous

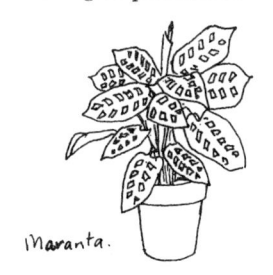

Maranta

Bushy

Hedera helix

Climbing

Dracaena

Upright

The all-time classic is the growing of an avocado seed. Plant it, small end up, in a pot of soil (either very close to the surface or leave the seed's tip exposed above the surface) and you will eventually have a beautiful foliage plant with large, green, almost-tropical leaves. A sweet potato will grow to become an attractive vine.

Most common of all are the small, shrub-like trees that are grown indoors from the seeds of citrus fruits—oranges, grapefruit, tangerines, limes, and lemons. Four or five seeds sown in six inch pot of soil will usually produce two or three sturdy little plants that often grow on to produce real fruit in time.

The top half-inch of a pineapple will root in a moist, sandy medium and can then be transplanted into a large container where it will grow and thrive as an interesting house plant. The seeds of dates will grow small palm trees. Some of the no-cost ideas require great patience, as these plants are often slow growers.

The containers that are used to hold plants can be almost anything from a discarded tea pot, coffee can, wash basin, or saucepan to the bowl-shaped skin of a half orange. In any case, it need not be costly.

Vegetables for the Apartment Gardener

Growing vegetables in containers is the way that vegetables can be grown by those who live in an apartment.

The modern cliff-dweller has no excuse for missing the enjoyment and benefit of growing his or her own vegetables. Little or no special equipment is required.

The new trend to growing plants of all kinds in containers has finally become fashionable for vegetables. Any kind of container that will hold soil and allow excess water to drain away will suffice as a container for growing delicious, fresh vegetables: bushel baskets; apple or fish boxes; old pails with drainage holes made in the bottom; buckets; large flower pots; discarded kitchen basins; pots and pans. The smaller containers are ideal for growing herbs such as parsley, sage, thyme, and for chives, radishes, green onions, leaf-lettuce and other greens as well. Larger containers may be used for growing the fruiting types of vegetables such as tomatoes, cucumbers, peppers, eggplants, onions, etc.

The apartment balcony and windowsill are perfect locations for vegetable containers, as are doorsteps and patios.

The Container Planting Medium

I suggest the following as a good mixture in which to grow container-held vegetables: one-third soil; one-third peat moss; one-third sand; and one cup of 8–8–7 fertilizer for each bushel of soil mixed. If you

Annual vines, such as morning glory and sweet peas, or vegetables, such as peas and beans, will grow in a container equipped with climbing supports.

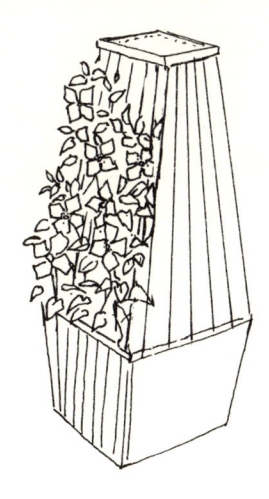

prefer, ready-bagged soils and soil mixtures are available at garden centres and nurseries.

When you fill the containers with the mixture be sure to place at least one inch of coarse sand or gravel in the bottom to assure good drainage. Where there are no drainage holes I suggest you make some; vegetables, perhaps, more than other plants, cannot survive if left standing in drenching soil.

Fertilizing the Container-held Vegetable Plants

I strongly urge you to keep some sort of records (such as a calendar) which will tell you when each feeding is required. Your first entry should be when the young vegetable plants have reached the two-leaf stage of growth. No sooner than three weeks *after* the plants reach the two-leaf stage, should fertilizer be applied, and then at three week intervals thereafter. Mix 8–8–7 fertilizer with the top half-inch of soil at the rate of one teaspoon per square foot of soil, *thoroughly watered in.* Water soluble fertilizer can also be applied (in place of the dry type) every second week at watering time. Dissolve one half teaspoon of fertilizer such as 20–20–20, or 10–52–10 in one gallon of water and then apply it to the soil.

Watering Container-grown Vegetables

Very careful attention should be given to the watering of container-held vegetable plants. As the soil becomes dry to one-half inch of the top, apply water enough to thoroughly wet the soil all the way to the bottom. Keep in mind that over-watering can kill the plants. Try not to allow water to splash the foliage.

Light Requirements

The most desirable situation for container-held vegetables is wide open, full sunlight, but some kinds will tolerate a little shade. The fruiting kinds of vegetables such as cucumbers, tomatoes and peppers need the most sunlight available. The leafy and root vegetables such as cabbage, lettuce, turnip, radishes, beets, etc. can survive in some shade.

Insect Control

No matter where vegetables are grown they will always be vulnerable to attack by insects, so be watchful for the earliest signs of this damage. For small infestations, the insects can be removed by hand, but when the insects persist and the infestation becomes more and more serious, use a recommended pesticide to save the vegetables from destruction.

Growing Vegetables the Easy Way

In all likelihood, the chief reason that many apartment-dwellers have avoided growing vegetables in their limited growing space is because they do not want to become involved in sowing seeds, transplanting, thinning out, etc. Vegetable gardening has been greatly simplified with the development of compressed peat pots (which are known by many different brand names on the market.) Nursery operators have taken just about every possible step to make the raising of vegetables as easy as can be. Without looking very far, the apartment gardener can now buy individually-potted vegetable plants in containers that can be plunged right into the soil, as is, without disturbing the soil in the container or the plant's roots. With this method, it is possible to enjoy almost 100 per cent success with vegetable transplants.

Started peat pots of vegetables also means the end of waste and overplanting. Instead of buying a whole package of cucumber seeds, when, for instance, all you need is three or four plants, you can now buy three or four started pots of cucumber with already-established roots and true leaves. This feature applies to many other varieties of vegetables. Indeed vegetables fresh from the garden are now within the easy reach of everyone, no matter where they live. I suggest you grow a few if only for the praise you will receive from guests enjoying tomato, cucumber, or lettuce, picked just seconds before they sit down to dinner. They might be delighted to pick their own.

Begonia   African Violet   Begonia

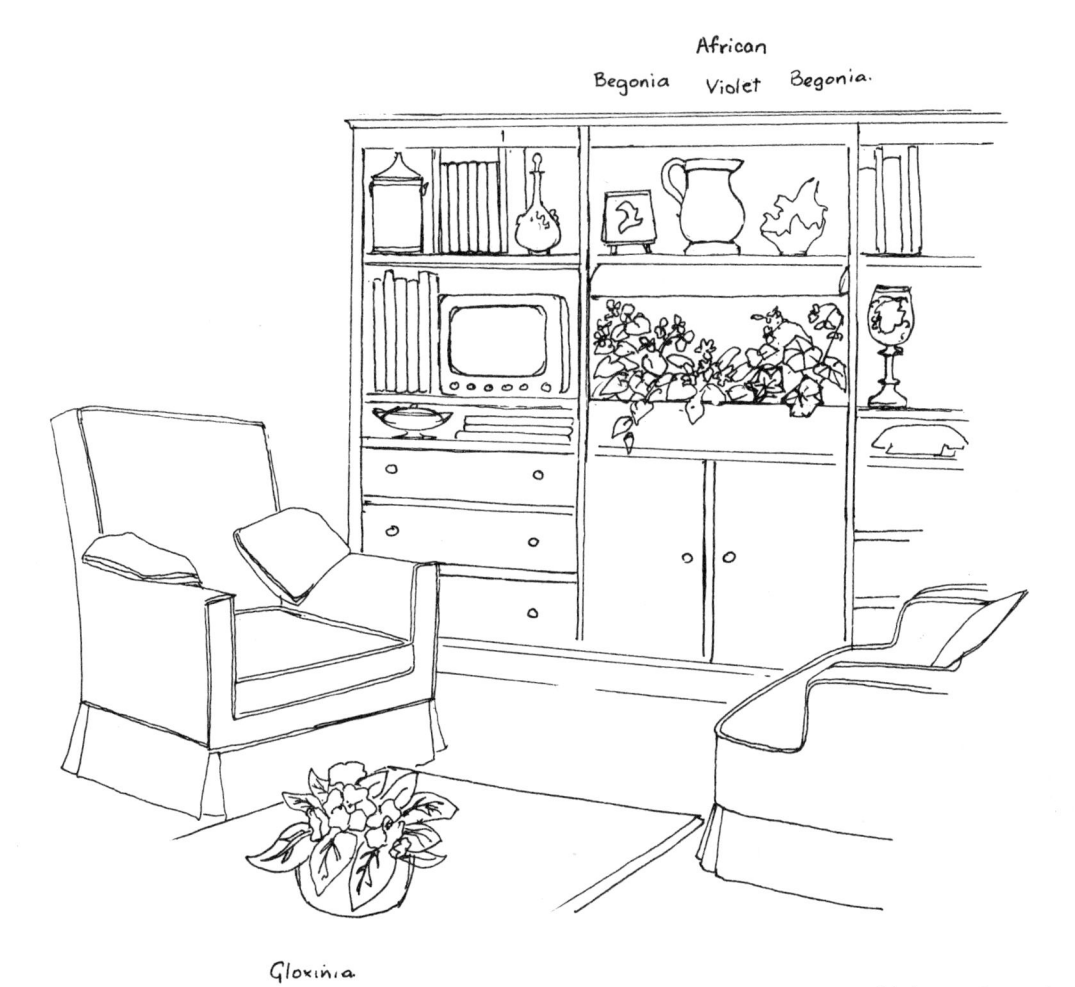

Gloxinia

Light garden built into wall unit

SUNLESS GARDENING

There once were people with a valid excuse for never having anything "alive and growing". Now, even those who live in quarters where there is not so much as a square foot of outdoor space, nor even a window to let in the sun, can still have a garden.

Floracart may be used for growing flowers, plants and vegetables.

The Fluorescent Fixture

The fluorescent light can assume the sun's energy-producing work. Growing plants under lights has become so popular in some places that there are clubs and societies of "gardening-under-lights" specialists who enjoy their own printed periodicals in which ideas, experiments and discoveries are exchanged.

Since with lights natural sunlight is unnecessary, this form of gardening can be undertaken anywhere—basement, crawl space, closet, or attic. Electrical manufacturers have produced beautiful and decorative fixtures suitable for use on end tables, book shelves, fireplace mantles, room dividers, desks and specially-made furniture. One, designed as a bracket lamp, would bring life and beauty to a dismal stairway.

In addition to decorative types, there are also the strictly functional light gardens assembled for the let's-get-down-to-business gardener. Ordinary fluorescent baffles and tubes installed in places where beauty of design is not essential will transform an attic into a tomato patch, a basement crawl space into an African violet plantation. Fluorescent light fixtures can be put to work growing fabulous displays of gloxinias and vividly-coloured achimenes, geraniums, and begonias.

In the space normally taken by a small dining room cabinet, a three-tiered, lighted flora cart may be placed, providing twenty-four square feet of growing space for plain and fancy, exotic or tropical plants. I have often taken particular pleasure in treating dinner guests to the delight of letting them pick their own fresh tomatoes directly from a 30-inch fluorescent planter situated near the dining room table. As the guests savour the delicious cherry-sized tomatoes they are also treated to a display of various flowering plants and a variety of young trees starting from seed right there at the tableside. They are always intrigued with the infant pines.

A dim corner at the end of a central hall in our home is cheerfully illuminated with a wall bracket-type planter, with its donut-shaped fluorescent tube and growing tray, just large enough for two small pots of African violet and a spray of trailing philodendron. An ordinary lamp

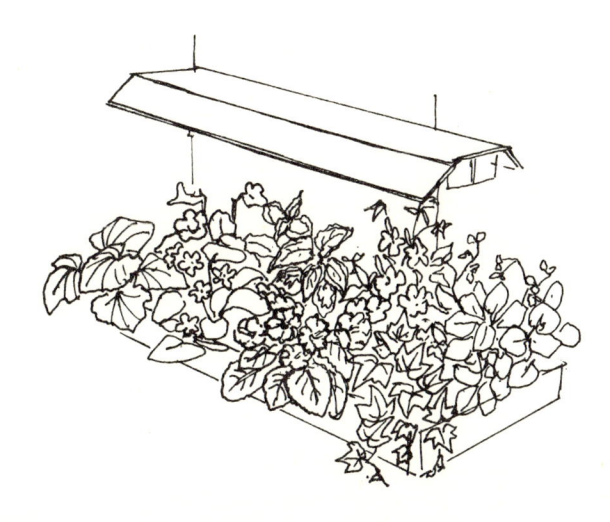

Typical single-tray light garden

might have been placed in this location, whereas now we have the benefits of both light fixture and vibrant flower colours.

Provided the plants are given the ordinary courtesy of watering and feeding when needed, they require very little care. Timers are available to see that the lights go on in the morning and off at night. People who started gardening under lights when no alternative form of gardening was available, now would not have it any other way. Even those who were completely indifferent in the beginning soon became enthralled with what can be accomplished. Those who have never planted anything in their lives find satisfaction by at first taking the easiest possible course —planting and forcing a few pots of flowering bulbs, such as daffodils, tulips, hyacinths, amaryllis and others. It is within the realm of possibility to actually grow your own orchids and all the gift plants you'd care to send your friends and you can grow them right in your own living room or in a corner of the basement.

Unusual and Novelty Plants Possible under Lights

The interest of younger members of a family will be held for longer than usual by novelty plants. One that never fails to arouse the interest (and the respect and care) of children is the plant that has the habit of "seeming" to come back from the dead. In its dry state the resurrection plant (*Selaginella lepidophylla*) looks just like a pale, green ball with no sign of life whatever. When you place it in a dish of water or in some damp soil, almost as if by magic it changes itself from a ball into a flat rosette. When the moisture has gone, the plant will gradually return to its former shape only to be resurrected again when water is re-applied.

The air plant (*Kalanchoe*), as its name suggests, will draw enough nourishment out of the air to grow and reproduce while left out of soil and without water! When pinned to a curtain, for example, it continues to perform to the amazement of viewers. While it is interesting in a dry state, if the air plant is given a proper home under the lights in some soil it will astound you with its versatility. Little plants will drop from the edges of the leaves and thrive in the moistness of a tray below covered with pebbles or vermiculite.

The very name voodoo lily (*Amorphophallus rivieri*) inspires visions of mysterious jungles in the imagination. When it produces its enormous brownish-red flower, with a dark, red rod rising from its center, the jungle image will be complete. In fairness, it should be noted that this plant often releases an unpleasant odor and may grow to a fabulous size and have to be moved outdoors. As it is a tropical plant and cannot tolerate cold, it must be brought back indoors long before danger of frost.

The autumn crocus produces beautiful flowers, and will actually flower while sitting on a windowsill without soil, but it will do much better when given a proper rooting medium in which to grow.

There are also plants definitely not for children. Sometimes called the wonder plants, the bulbous plants known as colchichums are poisonous and should be kept out of the reach of children and pets. The list of novel and unusual plants goes on. Check the plant lists and check with fellow-gardeners who will have personal favourites to recommend.

Water Gardens Under Lights

Some "light-gardening" is done in water and without soil. Fish tanks and aquariums, with or without a population of tropical fish, make the ideal container for the practice of "waterscaping". Where the full-sized aquarium garden is not desired, many different types of containers are used. Some aquatic gardeners grow plants in such things as large sea shells, brandy snifters, glass bricks, unusually-shaped bottles of all sizes, even large pickle bottles.

There is a large variety of plants that flourish in water and do equally well in soil. These include: coleus; pothos; nephthytis; philodendron; English ivy; and Chinese evergreen. They are started in water by knocking them from their pots and rinsing all soil from their roots (in water of room temperature). There are several means of holding the plants upright in the water one of which is a heavy-based holder containing non-rusting needle-like skewers on which the plants are thrust. Small ornaments of glass or glazed clay, or small stones or shells may also be used to hold the plants in place in the container. Add little pieces of charcoal to help keep the water sweet-smelling.

Aquarium Gardening Under Lights

The full-scale aquarium gardener generally starts out with a ten-gallon-sized tank, and usually also has a stock of tropical fish in the tank. When the agricultural types of fluorescent tubes are suspended above an aquarium the colours of the fish assume hues otherwise never seen. When there are no fish to be especially lighted for colour effect, the usual light formula for the aquarium consists of two 25 watt incandescent bulbs, or one 14 watt fluorescent tube. Some experts recommend the warm-white fluorescents for this purpose.

When the aquarium is placed in a location that is dark and cool the lights can be turned on for eight hours per day. When the tank is in the sunshine, or if algae forms too rapidly in any location, the number of hours of light or the size of the lights can be reduced.

The choice of plants for the aquarium is extensive. A few suggestions include: water sprite, hornwort, bacopa, hairgrass, banana plant, duckweed, and any of the new hybrid, small-growing water lilies. Other plants are named in the plant lists, particularly those lists that are released by nurseries specializing in water plants.

GARDENING AT THE OFFICE

According to sales figures the "light garden" concept has really caught on with the occupants of business and professional offices. Lobbies, waiting rooms, and reception areas have been made many times more attractive when "light gardens" have been installed. Business people soon learn that impatient clients seem to be made more at ease while waiting amid banks of colorful and fragrant living plants and flowers. Sales seem to go easier when the desk top is illuminated with a small lamp and a few pots of various-coloured begonias or other dainty flowers, instead of the usual blotter and pen set.

The office manager no longer has to choose between a potted palm and artificial foliage; now there is a choice between a tropical garden in each corner, a floral display on every desk, or a dozen flowering plants at the receptionist's desk.

Many of the newest office and commercial buildings, such as banks, the waiting rooms of airports, bus and train stations, enclosed shopping malls and so on, have special places where exotic plants thrive as living displays. Some architects now design modern working areas with self-sustaining, highly-illuminated plant enclosures where a wide array of plants live and multiply. Plants bring that touch of "aliveness" to what might be otherwise a totally inanimate cavern of concrete, glass and steel.

Light, Humidity and Temperature are Important

Desk top garden

Most large plants, of the types usually selected for offices, appreciate all the light that can be had. The overhead fluorescent lights used in the working areas of modern offices are usually ample to supply the needs of large tub-held foliage and tropical plants.

In areas dimly lit for special effect, such as reception areas, etc., the lack of light means that horticultural light fixtures must be used. Avoid the mistake of taking a plant that has stood in a dim corner for months and suddenly relocating it right in front of a sunny window. Make such a move gradually, shifting it a few feet closer to the light source each day over a period of several days.

In offices where extra humidity cannot be given to the plants, it is wise to avoid plants with hairy, soft, or thin foliage as these types usually demand much more humidity than others.

Unlike your own home or apartment, the office temperature is beyond your control. Temperature is usually controlled in such a way that it drops on weekends, or conversely, soars, causing the plants to become dry. The air conditioning equipment may be turned off Friday at quitting time and not started up again until Monday morning. Plants in older buildings often suffer drafty locations; others must contend with excessive dust.

Take Care with Watering

Quite often the plants at the office decline gradually because they are given either far too much or too little water. Different people think the plant needs watering at varying times. This results in too much water given too often, although light sprinkling of dusty leaves is probably always welcome for most plants.

Although it is almost impossible to recommend a certain method and time of watering plants at the office, there is one general rule which is fairly safe to observe. The rule—when the soil is dry and hard to the touch, water the plant well, and leave it until the soil is again dry and hard to the touch. If in doubt as to whether the plants need water yet, wait one more day and then apply the water. It is very possible that some offices are so warm and dry that the plants will require water twice a week.

Plants that Tolerate Office Conditions

The most logical type of plant to seek out for the office is the tropical foliage type that withstands high and low, and fluctuating temperatures, and poor lighting and low humidity. Most flowering plants require a cool temperature and high humidity. Three plants that are known to be reliable in the adverse growing conditions of an office are:

1. The rubber plant (*Ficus elastica*) with tall stems and large, green, lanceolate leaves. The rubber plant also has a variegated leaf variety that is very attractive and should be welcome in any office setting.
2. The snake plant, sometimes also called mother-in-law's tongue, (*Sansevieria*) originates in the tropical zones of India and Africa. It features rigid, spearlike leaves that rise straight up from the soil without branches or stems. In addition to the pure-green forms there are also variegated types with creamy strips along the edge of the leaves.
3. The cast iron plant (*Aspidistra lurida*) is the plant that song-star Gracie Fields made popular during World War Two singing about "The Biggest Aspidistra In the World". This plant offers large, wide, strap-like leaves which arise from the root at ground level. These leaves grow to about twenty to twenty-four inches in height and maintain a good, solid-green colour.

Figs also perform well in the conditions of the typical office and deserve your attention when you are selecting the plant to decorate where you work. Figs (*Ficus*) offer a variety of leaf form. The fiddle-leaved

Hand sprayer for applying chemicals or water sprays to indoor and balcony plants. Offices especially tend to be very dry in winter.

fig (*Ficus lyatra*) has large leaves in the shape of a violin. The weeping fig (*Ficus benjamina*) is similar to fiddle-leaves fig but has smaller and wavy-margined leaves. The variety "Exotica", the Java fig, is even more refined and graceful of form. Mistletoe fig (*Ficus diversifolia*) has tiny leaves and a twiggy form which is especially suited to the hard growing conditions of the office.

Plants for Poor Light Conditions

In those offices where it is impossible to provide a good, bright light, grow umbrella trees. The umbrella trees, also called the scheffleras, somehow manage to live in the most arid conditions even where only low light-intensity is available. Although they actually thrive with good light, they will grow satisfactorily in poor light. All three varieties of the umbrella trees offer big, palmately-compound, umbrella-like leaves.

Other low-light plants include several of the palms, including, the large lady palm (*Rhapis excelsa*), which features the typical fan-shaped leaves and an overall bamboo-like appearance, with the built-in ability to tolerate a lot of abuse. The sentry palm (*Howea belmoreana*) and the paradise palm (*Howea forsteriana*) also seem to survive in low light and low humidity.

Plants for Drafty Places with Changing Temperatures

In those chilly offices, and particularly the lobbies and entrances where the temperatures are likely to fluctuate from normal to very cold to almost freezing at times, and where the light intensity is often extremely low, one of the handsome laurels will survive. The aucuba laurel (*Aucuba japonica*) is recommended for lobbies. Where the temperatures often go from quite cool to very warm the philodendrons are often recommended. Select from ceriman, *Philodendron pertusum*, *Philodendron sellowianum*, and *Philodendron hastatum*.

BOTTLE, TERRARIUM & DISH

Several kinds of plant containers are possible in one room. Window planter provides basic theme, others are shape and colour accents.

Briefly, *bottle gardening* is a tiny garden growing inside a bottle.

Start with a clear glass bottle (preferably one with a wide neck) that is scrupulously clean. If a chemical glass cleaner has been used on the inside, wipe it out with a spray and a lintless cloth (which can be held on a twisted wire) and allow a day for the fumes to ventilate before starting the planting.

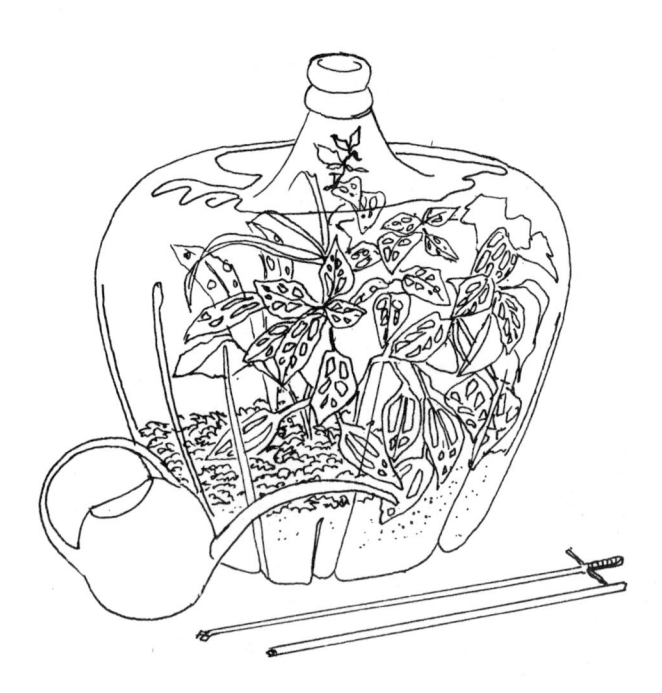

A bottle garden

The rain cycle in a terrarium

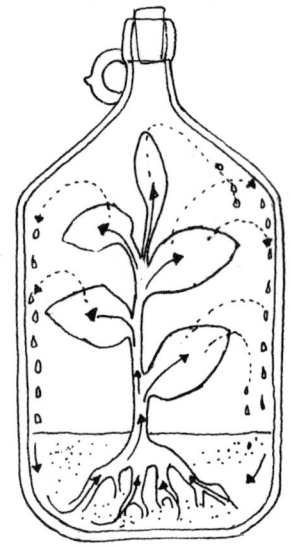

- - -→ Evaporated moisture
- ο ο ο Condensation
- → Moisture absorbed by plant

A *terrarium* is a covered, enclosed miniature garden. An *open terrarium* is a miniature garden in a container such as a brandy snifter. An open terrarium technically becomes a "true" terrarium only when it is given some sort of lid and thereby will contain moisture within. Open containers cannot maintain a "rain cycle" and must be frequently watered. As well they are vulnerable to disease and insects. Open terrariums do, however, permit the gardener to plant from among a larger choice of plants which do not require constantly high humidity.

The bottle garden and the terrarium, once planted will set up their own "rain cycle" and will seldom, if ever, need to be watered.

The miniature dish garden is also, just as its name implies, a small garden planted in a dish (of any size). Unlike the terrarium and bottle garden, the dish garden does require watering quite often, whenever the soil becomes dry.

The *light requirements* for these three types of indoor gardens depend on the types of plants that you place in them. If you plant sun-loving plants in your dish garden, then obviously they must be placed in a spot where at least a minimum amount of sunlight will play on them.

The bottle garden and terrarium should never be placed in direct sunlight or they will overheat and scald the plants. If the plants you select are those that have variegated foliage or those that produce flowers, they will certainly require more light than other plants.

If you cannot provide a location in a diffused light situation, remember that the direct sun never shines in a north window and so this amount of exposure would be just fine. The interior design of the room

An open-topped terrarium and a dish garden

where the terrarium or bottle garden will live may dictate that you must sit your plants in a dim corner; they could be moved to good light for about ten hours every day, or you could place a horticultural light over them.

Wherever you choose to place your bottle garden or terrarium, be sure that the plants enclosed will not suffer the ravages of drastic temperature changes. Such plants readily adapt to the constant temperature of your home but cannot tolerate sudden or drastic changes of heat.

As already stated, the true terrarium must have a lid, or some sort of seal over the opening in order to get the "rain cycle" into operation and for it to continue to function. Bottle gardens do not need to be sealed as very little moisture will escape through the narrow neck of the bottle. However, they can be sealed and opened only when the condensation ceases to form on the glass interior and rewatering is necessary.

The amount of actual soil needed to start a terrarium, bottle, or dish garden, is so minimal that it hardly seems to make sense for you to go about mixing your own. I suggest you buy a plastic bag of prepared soil, knowing that will be fumigated against insects and sterilized against diseases and will contain just the right amount of soil ingredients necessary to the good health of your miniature garden plants.

You will also need some horitcultural charcoal and small pebbles or gravel. You may find these ingredients in a store that sells aquarium supplies if it is not available elsewhere. The sketch will indicate how to layer these ingredients in your container.

Note that you *do not* need to *fertilize* your miniature gardens. Most

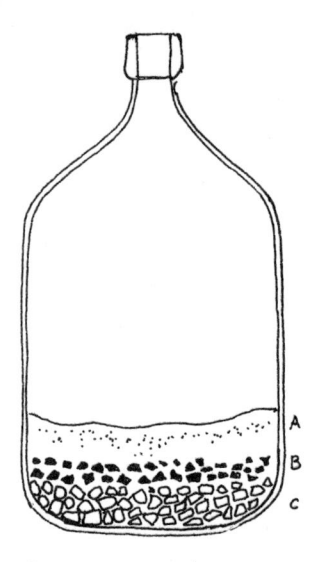

A. Potting mixture
B. Charcoal
C. Drainage Material (crushed rock, broken clay pots or pebbles)

of the plants chosen for such containers (never use outdoor plants from your garden) will adapt to terrarium conditions immediately and fertilizer will only unnecessarily speed up growth. Fertilized terrarium plants tend to quickly outgrow the container and become unattractive. Plants may also suffer fertilizer burn in a container.

The following is a list of twenty-four plants for use in *terrariums, bottle gardens, dish gardens,* and *open terrariums*. Shown, will be the plant's common name, its botanical name, its heat tolerance (room temperature), humidity and light requirements. Unless otherwise stated, all plants will be adaptable to the four types of planters listed above. Where the word "accessible" appears it will indicate that the plant needs to be in a container which allows for a reasonable amount of room for you to prune it or remove dead or unwanted foliage.

Japanese sweet flag (*Acorus gramineus variegatus*), 55° F., high humidity, bright light.
Maidenhair fern (*Adiantum*), 60° F., high humidity, shade, accessible.
Aglaonema. 60° F., low moisture, dim, accessible.
Bugleweed (*Ajuga reptans*), (not in terrariums or bottle gardens) 65° F., low humidity, bright light.
Joseph's coat (*Alternanthera bettzickiana*), 60° F., medium humidity, bright light, accessible.

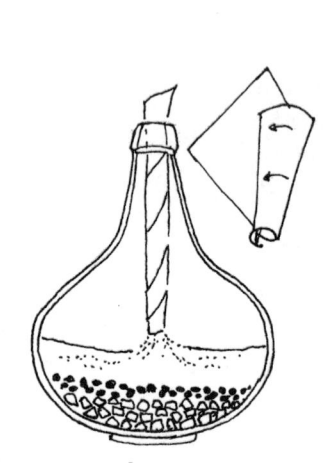

Paper cone for adding soil

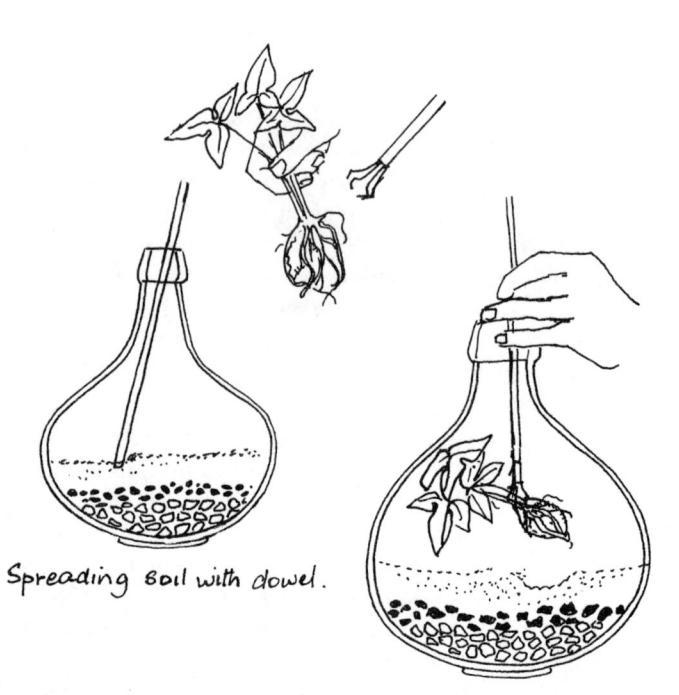

Spreading soil with dowel.

Terrarium planting procedure

Planting

80

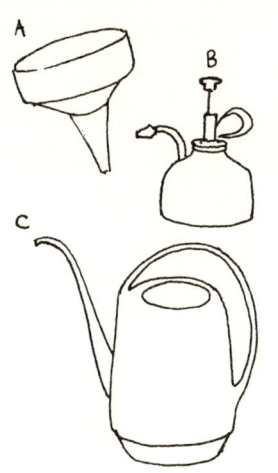

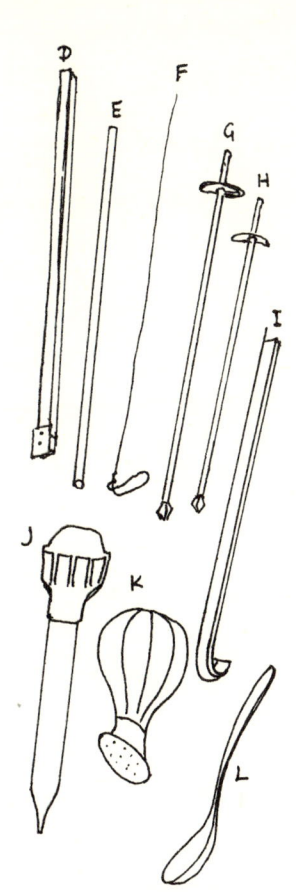

Various tools for bottle and terrarium gardening. Many can easily be improvised.

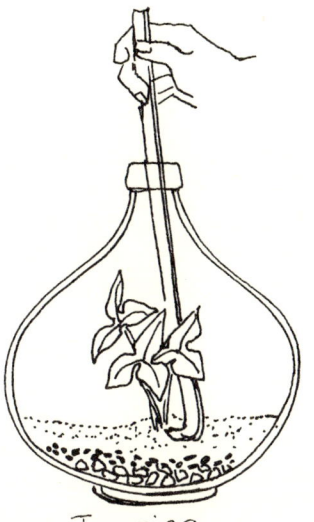

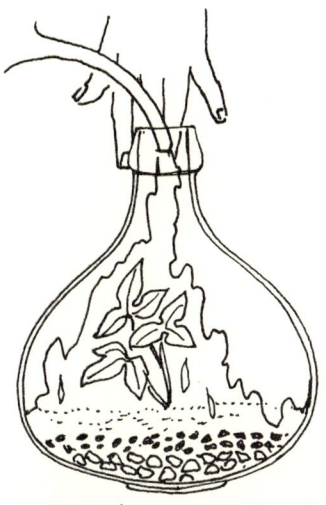

A. Funnel
B. Mist Sprayer
C. Watering Can.
D. Pruning-stick-razor blade on end.
E. Dowel   F. Looped wire
G + H. Pick-up tools
I. Plexiglass Tamping Tool
J. Baster
K. Bulb-Type water sprayer
L. Spoon.

Tamping

Watering.
(Spread water down inside by pouring over fingers.)

81

Flowering bulbs in container make an attractive display.

Pig-tail plant (*Anthurium scherzerianum*), 80° F., high humidity, partial shade.

Aphelandra squarrosa 60° F., high humidity, diffused light, accessible.

Coralberry (*Ardisia crenata*), (not for dish gardens) 50° F., high humidity, light shade.

Asparagus fern (*Asparagus ornamental*), 45° F., low humidity, diffused light, accessible. There are several excellent varieties.

Cast-iron plant (*Aspidistra lurida*), (for large containers only) 45° F., high humidity, shade.

Spleenwort (*Asplenium*), 50° F., high humidity, lower in winter, diffused light. There are many varieties.

Japanese aucuba (*Aucuba japonica*), 40° F., high humidity, diffused light.

Begonia. There are hundreds of species. Be sure to buy only dwarf kinds. 75° F., medium humidity, diffused light.

Bromeliad. There are many species; 60° F., low humidity, filtered bright light.

Fancy-leafed caladium (*Caladium bicolor*), 75° F., low humidity, partial shade, accessible.

Maranta (*Calathea*), 55° F., medium humidity, filtered sunlight, (not for dish garden).

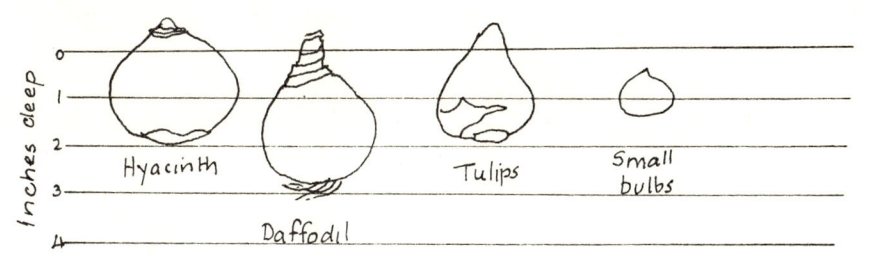

Correct depths for planting bulbs

Holly fern (*Cyrtomium falcatum*), (not for dish gardens) 50° F., low humidity, medium-bright light.
Peacock plant (*Episcia cupreata*), 65° F., high humidity, partial shade.
Velvet plant (*Gynura aurantiaca*), 70° F., high humidity, strong light, accessible.
Prayer plant (*Maranta leuconeura kerchoviana*), (not for dish gardens) 65° F., low humidity, strong light.
Rabbit tracks (*Maranta leuconeura*), 65° F., high humidity, filtered sunlight.
Pygmy date palm (*Phoenix roebelenii*), 50° F., medium humidity, good light.
Miniature Rose (*Rosa chinensis* 'Minima'). Many varieties, (not for dish gardens), 50° F., high humidity, any light—requires daily airing.
Mother-of-thousands (*Saxifraga sarmentosa*), 60° F., low humidity, filtered light.

There are dozens and dozens of other plants that are suitable for growing in terrarium-like conditions and can be easily found by searching the catalogues and plant lists of "specialist houses" which sell only these kinds of plants.

Plant cuttings in terrarium benefit from a period of time under lights.

TOOLS

Buy quality tools and equipment. I strongly suggest that you do not look for bargains in gardening equipment and tools unless you are certain that the items offered are reduced in price in a genuine sale. Especially in gardening equipment you only get what you pay for. I also urge you to buy only the tools and equipment needed. A poorly made tool or the wrong tool is worse than none.

Qualities To Look For In Tools

Check the wood in the handles and be certain that it is of a good quality hardwood that is likely to stand up against splintering and splitting when put to heavy work. Try to obtain tools with a water-resistant finish so that equipment will be protected if left out in the weather, by mistake. Make sure that the handle and metal parts are solidly fastened together. Often in small tools, the wooden handles are squeezed or bashed into a metal tube or pipe only to become loose and fall out as soon as the wood ages and dries.

All metal parts should be good quality. The teeth in rakes should be strong enough to resist bending and yet have some spring to them. Hoes, spades and other cutting edges should be able to hold a good sharp edge and be as chip-resistant as possible. It is a waste of money to buy less than good quality tools and equipment, or to buy tools and gadgets that you will never use.

One of the most valuable tools for indoor use is a hand mister for spraying or syringing plant foliage. Another important indoor item is a small-sized, long-necked watering can. Tools for loosening soil in flower pots and other planters can range all the way from a wooden stick to a kitchen knife. Few, if any, other indoor garden tools are required.

THE COMPOST HEAP

In the natural way of things absolutely nothing goes to waste. When plants are finished with their stems, leaves, stalks, roots, flowers and seed containers, they are turned over to nature's industrious wonder-workers, the decomposers. These are the tiny creatures that work tirelessly at chewing, digesting, and passing through their systems all the plant material that is of no other use. They are responsible for the manufacture of humus, which is the main ingredient in growth-sustaining soil. The decomposers will willingly go to work for any gardener who invites them to come and live in his compost heap.

The compost heap will be of great value to the home gardener, as an excellent source of priceless organic material for improving and conditioning garden soils. It is a handy place to dispose of all organic waste such as: grass clippings; discarded fruit and vegetables; peelings; dead foliage; weeds (that have *not* gone to seed); the tops of dead annual and perennial plants; straw; manure; turf trimmings; leaves; soil left over from holes dug for planting—whatever is organic matter. The decomposers will work their magic on it and transform refuse into valuable compost. Although woody materials take considerably longer than softer materials to break down, they too can be composted when the gardener is willing to wait.

A compost heap is a worthwhile project no matter what size the garden. Gardeners with more spacious, suburban and rural grounds can afford the space that a large compost heap demands and there may even be easy access to the needed materials such as straw, corn stalks, and so on.

Even in small places the compost bin can be hidden by growing plants.

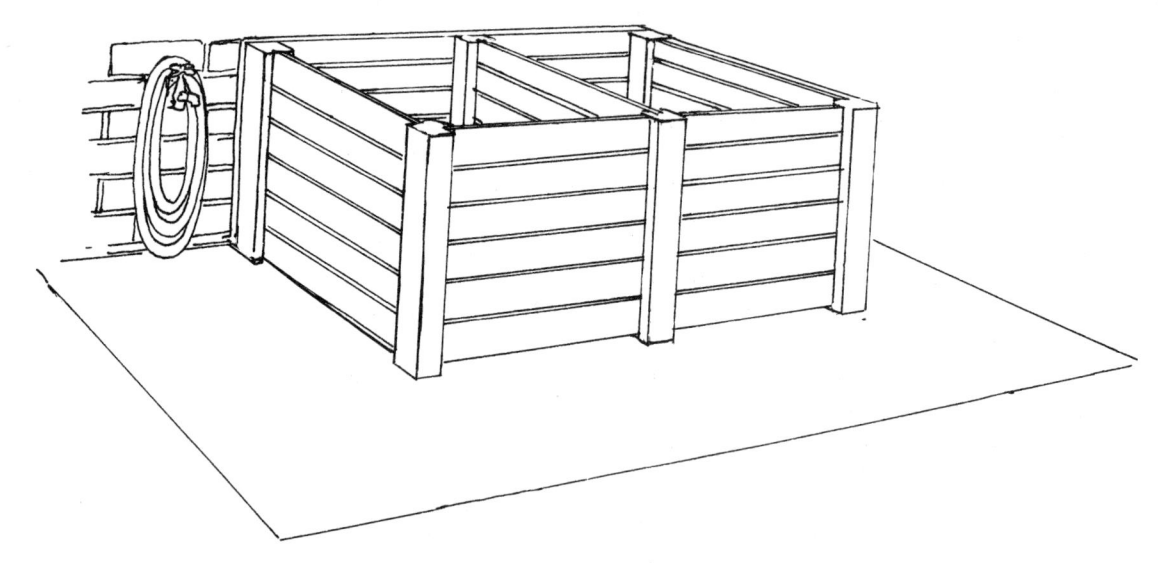

Two-compartment compost bin has removable ends.

The Small-scale Compost Heap

Downtown, the gardener is more limited in space and in his or her choice of composting materials; nevertheless, compost can be kept in some sort of container. You will find ready-made compost containers on the market; some come complete with catalytic starters to speed up the process. An old wash tub or ash can will make a practical container. A wooden box will not last because the decomposition process affects its wood as well as twigs and grass and the box will soon need to be replaced.

In an out-of-the-way corner of the garden—say an area three feet square—make a low retaining wall about two feet high. A few boards nailed together would do for walls with the earth for a floor. Into this bin, dump your organic waste—everything from grass clippings and gardening trimmings to coffee grounds and tea leaves. There is sometimes an odor from the heap and so it should be located remote from windows and doors.

If you cannot spare three feet of space for such a container, simply pile up the waste material behind a shrub, against a fence, or even in a garbage pail. The waste will eventually reduce itself in size until the compost reaches a state when it can be dug into the garden to enrich the soil. Materials left piled from fall to spring will be all right to dig in as a soil conditioner but the compost will be of more use to your plants when it is thoroughly decomposed.

The Pill

Whatever form of compost heap you choose nature can be assisted in the work of decomposition by chemicals. Visit your garden center or nursery and ask for a chemical decomposer. This is usually available in the form of pills to be dissolved in water and sprinkled over the heap. The chemical speeds up the process of decomposition and also helps to reduce odor. Safe to use, they are also often quite inexpensive.

Whether or not you use chemical aids, some materials take longer than others to break down. Oak leaves are very slow and, since they are often available in large quantities, they serve better as a mulch or for use as a protective winter covering over tender plants than as compost. Oak leaves may be run through a shredder and dug back into the soil in a merely squashed condition to decompose in their own good time.

Evergreen needles, twigs, branches and other forms of woody material are also very slow to decompose. If you have space enough for two heaps, one could hold fast decaying compost and the other could hold the woody stuff which takes a longer time to break down.

Large Compost Heaps

For those who have room and sufficient waste material to dispose of, here are two ways to make a full-size compost heap.

Method number one. Take your choice, either dig a hole approximately four feet by six feet and about six inches deep, or, construct a pit of stone of the same size with the walls extending two feet high. With this system the walled pit probably gives the best results, the only drawback being that a drainage outlet in one corner must be provided. Where there is drainage to carry off excess liquid, there must also be somewhere provided for the run-off juices to go.

When the hole or walled pit are ready for use, start in with a foot-deep layer of straw, or other bulky organic material such as corn stalks, thus allowing air circulation and good drainage at the bottom of the heap. Next pile on a six-inch layer of weeds, refuse, sods, etc. lightly packed. Apply water until thoroughly wet. Sprinkle on a fertilizer that has an analysis of a high nitrogen content which will help in the organic breakdown. Next, add one or two inches of soil to complete the layer. Build up layer on layer in this manner, tapering the pile. Form a depression in the top to hold moisture in dry weather. In wet weather the pile edges should be rounded to help moisture run-off. In the very hot weather apply water enough to keep the pile moist but not soggy.

If the pile becomes too tightly packed, use a crowbar or some other pointed object to punch holes into the center of the pile to allow better air circulation. The pile will need to maintain the high temperatures that are needed for composting during the winter and so it should be given a good thick mulch of leaves or straw. The mulch will also help prevent it from drying out. Again, it is usually better to build two piles— one for ready use, the other for the future, when advanced decomposition has taken place.

Method number two. With this method, the compost pile should be about five feet high and six feet wide. The size depends on the amount of composting the gardener expects to do, and so provision is made for possible extension. When both ends are left open the fresh material can be applied to one end while the decomposed stuff can be removed from the other.

The material used in constructing the sides of the compost pile depends on what is available. Often the side walls are made of loosely placed concrete blocks which can be moved as necessary to allow for expansion of the pile. Another popular means of building side walls is to set wood planks on edge between two closely placed posts that have been sunk in the ground at each corner. Obviously, the walls are kept loose and movable in both cases.

Start the pile with a foot-thick layer of straw, or other coarse organic matter, allowing for air circulation and good moisture drainage. Next apply a six-inch layer of green waste with a sprinkling of a complete fertilizer (at the rate of 200 pounds per ton of compost). With the fertilizer also apply a sprinkling of lime. The lime and fertilizer help to break down the organic matter; lime also helps keep the heap odor-free.

Continue building such layers, adding green waste, sod bits, refuse, etc., in sandwich-like fashion until the six-foot height has been reached. Make a dip in the top of the pile to catch water, remembering that the pile must be kept moist during dry weather. A sheet of four or six mil polyethylene holds in moisture, helps decomposition, and prevents odor.

Turn the material at least once during the decomposing period to move the materials at the outer edges into the centre where more rapid decomposition occurs.

Using the Compost Material

When the gardener is sure that the organic matter on the pile has been thoroughly broken down and that it has lost all solid and fibrous matter, the compost can be taken directly from the pile and placed right on the garden. There is no need to wait once decomposition has taken place. It is sometimes necessary to shake the compost through a quarter-inch sieve to remove all stones and bits of woody material when it is to be used for the purpose of top-dressing the lawn.

MULCH

Mulches can be a great help. The experienced gardener is almost always quick to agree that mulching saves hours and hours of work while helping to produce a much better garden. The main purposes of mulches are to end the need for cultivating the soil; to gradually build up the humus content of the soil; to conserve moisture; to lessen the need for weeding; to lower the soil temperature during extremely hot weather; and to basically assist in better plant growth.

What is a mulch? Materials used as mulches in the garden are almost as varied as their purposes. Mulch is usually any kind of fibrous material that is low in price and readily available and which can be spread over the entire surface of the garden, or around individual plants, to about four inches deep. The most common mulches include—straw; hay; wood shavings; sawdust; peat moss; wood chips; shredded bark; decayed leaves; cocoa-bean shells; oat hulls; buckheat hulls; corn cobs. Sheet plastic is now widely used to mulch such plants as tomatoes and strawberries. Also used is sphagnum moss, shredded paper, and other materials.

Mulch is a Work Saver

Once all the plants are set in the garden for the year and they have become well established (usually by the second or third week of June) it is the time apply about four inches of a mulch material. It can either be placed over the entire garden bed, leaving only the plants poking through, or the mulch can be placed around each individual plant. It is next to impossible for anything (including weeds) to emerge from the soil and penetrate four inches of mulch to reach the sunlight. Therefore, mulching almost guarantees a weed-free garden.

Cultivating the garden to prevent the surface from getting hard packed and crusty is, after weeding, the hardest job. Mulching eliminates the need for cultivating as the soil remains cool and moist beneath the mulch material. In fact, the soil is also constantly gaining more humus content.

Handling Mulch Materials

Sawdust and wood shavings are sometimes easy to get from woodworking shops and sawmills, and while both are slow decomposers, they will draw a great deal of the plant's supply of nitrogen from the soil

Mulching must not touch tree trunk

and so extra nitrogen must be applied. Apply a dressing of high nitrogen fertilizer to the area before applying woody mulches such as sawdust and wood shavings, or smaller and fewer flowers will be the result.

Other woody mulches, that require extra nitrogen added to the soil, include wood chips, peat moss and corn cobs. A compost heap onto which a good amount of leaves has been deposited makes a most acceptable mulch material. Be sure to keep straw or woody mulches moistened to avoid the possibility of their catching fire.

Plastic Mulches

Because plastic is inorganic and will not readily decompose, it will not improve the structure of the soil by adding humus content, but it will do all the other things for which the organic mulches are used. Plastic will reduce the need for cultivating and weeding and will conserve moisture.

Before anything is planted, black polyethylene sheets are spread over the entire garden area completely covering the soil. Slits are cut to allow existing plants to poke through. When planting additional material in the garden a new slit is made and the plant inserted in the soil beneath in the traditional manner. Clods of soil, or stones, or small weights of any kind are sometimes needed to hold the plastic in place.

When contemplating a tomato patch or a strawberry patch, be sure to include strips of polyethylene in your plans. You will soon realize what a benefit this is. Tomato plants suffer in various ways when subjected to long periods of drought and alternating periods of very wet followed by very dry. The polyethylene sheets retain moisture and help keep the plants continually drought-free.

Strawberries benefit from a plastic mulch. Strawberries have the habit of sending runners along the ground which root themselves at intervals and send out still more runners to still more plants. When allowed to grow randomly strawberries would soon form a complete and dense matting over a broad area (far beyond the boundaries of the strawberry patch). By planting strawberry plants through slits made in a sheet of plastic spread over the bed the runnering habit can be controlled, as only plants in desirable locations are given a slit in the plastic and all others are removed. The growth habits of strawberries obviously can make weeding a major problem, but it is one that can be almost eliminated with polyethylene sheets.

SOIL

Know and understand your soil. These days it is so simple for the apartment gardener, or the downtown gardener with a very small space to obtain all the soil she or he will need for success with plants. Insect-free and disease-free soil for all purposes is sold in convenient plastic bags of from two to fifty pounds in size.

Those who find it totally impractical to buy soil to make a whole garden need to know some basic soil facts, so that good results may be had by improving the soil available. No matter what you plant you must be aware that success in gardening depends very much on the soil. There is a spectacular difference in soils; they vary from heavy, dense, almost nonporous clays, to light sands. Many are entirely useless for gardening purposes until improvements have been made.

Where the soil is sandy the garden is easy to work but water drains out too quickly and the soil dries out very fast. This type must be improved with ample amounts of organic matter to give it water-holding capacity. At an opposite extreme the clays are slower in drying, and hold their mineral content longer, but are very hard to work.

Ideal Soil

The ideal home garden soil would consist of 40 per cent humus, 40 per cent clay, and 20 per cent sand.

Care given the soil shows up in the results achieved in the garden. When the physical condition of the soil is improved and the fertility kept at an acceptable level, the gardener is greatly rewarded by a bountiful harvest. On the other hand, when soil is left as is and its conditioning ignored, your plants may be sickly and unattractive.

Applying fertilizer does not always mean that the problem of obtaining good soil is eliminated. Fertilizers on their own do not make productive soil. Many elements are involved. The amount of organic matter that the soil contains, its composition and texture, its acidity or alkalinity, its drainage and the amount of compaction it has received are all significant factors in determining the productivity of the soil.

Organic Matter is a Must

Before good crops can be expected the soil must have a good content of organic matter or humus. Organic substances increase the soil's water-retaining ability, and at the same time, help with good drainage. Oxygen

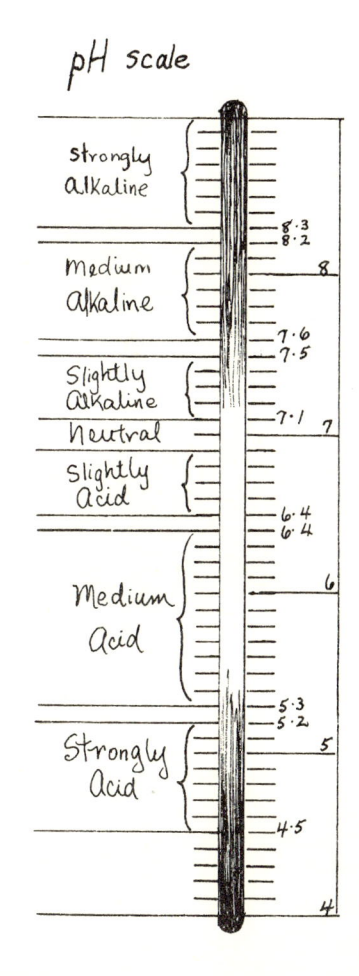

pH scale

Strongly alkaline
8.3
8.2
Medium alkaline — 8
7.6
7.5
Slightly alkaline
7.1 — 7
Neutral
Slightly acid
6.4
6.4
Medium acid — 6
5.3
5.2
Strongly acid — 5
4.5
4

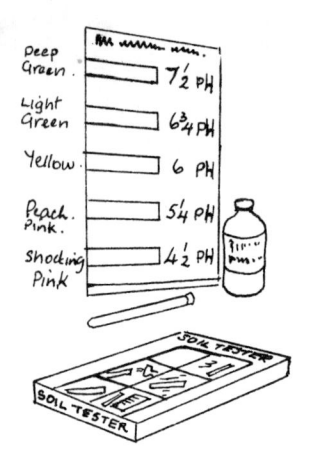

A soil test will show the p^H of your soil and indicate remedial ingredients.

is given passage into the soil and waste gases seep out. When organic material is present in the soil valuable nutrients are held in place and not allowed to leach (or flush) away as the moisture departs.

Good Drainage is Required

Satisfactory drainage can be achieved even in some of the toughest, densest clay soils when some means of physical improvement is made to allow water penetration and flow. The addition of such inorganic materials as coarse sand, gravel, well-washed coal ashes, or vermiculite helps break down the denseness of the clay particles and opens tiny channels through which moisture and air can penetrate. Some organic materials such as very coarse peat moss, strawy manure, or plain straw will also go a long way towards opening up a heavy soil.

If the soil is so dense and is so badly drained the water takes a very long time to seep, or drain away, even after you have made the physical improvements described above, tile drainage may be needed. If you believe that this remedy is required, I suggest you call in an expert and let him do the work for you.

Why Bother to Fertilize?

Plant foods, or fertilizers, supply the nutrients that plants must have if they are to survive. We should always remember that every plant must have the proper diet with which to thrive.

There are two basic kinds of fertilizers—organic and inorganic. Organic fertilizers are those such as animal waste (manure), bonemeal, bloodmeal, and decayed vegetable matter (compost). All of these supply nutrients to the soil as they slowly decompose, and they need the action of bacteria before they can be taken by the feeder roots of plants.

Inorganic fertilizers are almost always made by man and usually come in a form that can be used directly by the plant without passing through the decomposing process. Those are usually cheaper than organic fertilizers, but they must be carefully applied—never over-applied—as they will burn the roots and foliage and ruin the plants.

There are also modern synthetic fertilizers, such as those called urea, which are related to the inorganic fertilizers. These synthetics decompose slowly and supply a very large, steady supply of nitrogen, often as much as forty-five percent, and have the advantage of not burning the plants.

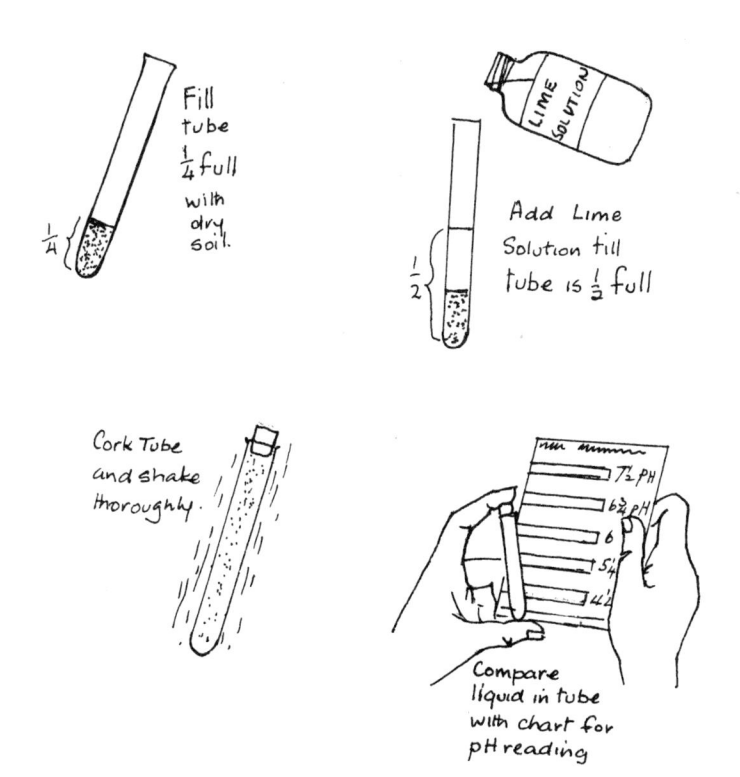

The soil test is easily carried out. Other kits are available to test for the presence of various necessary elements.

Soil Tests Usually Tell All

All plants need a balanced diet composed chiefly of the elements: nitrogen, phosphates, and potash. The amount of each of these three main ingredients in the package is always indicated on the label, expressed as numbers: 5–10–15; 7–7–7; 8–8–6; 7–10–5. These numbers are always listed in the same order; the first refers to the nitrogen content, the second to phosphates, and the third to potash.

Sometimes more of one element than another is missing from the soil, and to compensate for this shortage, more of the missing chemical must be added. A fertilizer with the appropriate formula to correct the imbalance will be the one with its highest number for the missing element.

Without a soil test it is just guess work and you will not know what is needed (unless you are an experienced gardener and can recognize deficiency symptoms). Perhaps the more important information that you will get from a soil test is the pH rating of the soil on your property. The pH is the amount of acidity or alkalinity present in the soil. Some plants (such as heath plants) thrive in soil with a high pH, while others must have a low reading.

When the test shows that the soil is too acid, the laboratory or the soil test kit will indicate the amount of limestone that should be added to correct for this lack. Experienced soil experts can often tell by simply looking at the soil and at the kinds of plants that are thriving, whether or not limestone is required.

For example, where such wild plants as orange hawkweed or wild strawberry live, the soil is almost always high in acidity and requires an application of limestone. When the soil-test shows that the soil is not acid enough, an application of chelated iron, or sulphur, will help correct the situation.

I cannot state the various amounts of which pH soil-conditioning ingredients will be needed as only each individual soil test will tell you these figures. To get better results with whatever you grow it is worth putting your soil to this test.

Soil test kits are usually available wherever garden supplies and accessories are sold and are not expensive (usually less than three dollars). Take a few minutes to carefully read the instructions and you will find the soil test kits are quite convenient for home gardeners to operate on their own.

Heavy Clay

In the section on drainage, it is mentioned that clay usually requires some additions and improvements. Something must be done so that moisture can pass through the soil. Adding organic and (or) inorganic materials definitely improves both drainage and the water-retaining capacity of clay soils. When given a chance, nature will greatly assist in this task as fallen leaves, bits of bark or whatever, add humus.

Drying out the soil for spring planting is one of the main problems connected with a heavy clay soil. Letting nature help is always the least expensive way of doing things. Spring is the time for you to dig or till the garden, even though the soil is far too wet to be used as a seedbed.

Depending on the space you have to work with, dig it to spade depth in strips thirty-six to forty-eight inches wide, leaving a narrower undug strip. You can then work the soil by stepping on the undug strips. Turn the soil over and leave the wet, lumpy soil just as the spade turned it, without breaking up the clods. Soil experts have proved that the soil in those opened rows, or beds, exposed to the rays of the early spring sunshine, will warm up by fifteen to twenty degrees while the temperature of the surrounding undug soil will rise only two or three degrees.

The next move is very important in the breaking down of clay soils in the home garden. Prevent the newly-dug, lumpy soil from shrinking and baking under the sun by periodically breaking the lumps with a rake. On bright days only a few hours of sunshine are needed before the first break-up treatment with the rake is practical, and often by the end of a sunny day the seedbed is ready for use. When the weather stays cool and wet it may require several days for the soggy clods of clay to be broken down and made friable.

When you are satisfied that the strips, or beds, are suitably broken down, then give the same treatment to those undug strips.

Ideally, hard-to-work-with clay soils are best broken down when we use both of the above recommended practices: (1) Work and dig in some sand and/or organic matter; (2) Dig and till carefully early in the spring so that the seedbed can be warmed as much as possible in advance of spring planting.

Soils for Seedlings

Whether you have a large-scale garden or are using only a collection of various and sundry flower pots and containers, you will need the right kind of soil. I have already stated that it is a simple matter to purchase various soils for all gardening needs in any quantity you desire from two pounds to two tons. Of course, the best way "to get the feel of the soil" is to mix your own. You may find that mixing your own soil is an activity that will give you the most satisfaction from gardening. However you go about it, if the tiny, delicate seeds you sow are going to have a fighting chance to germinate and grow they will require the right combination of moisture, oxygen and soil temperature.

Here is what I suggest as the proper soil recipe for good seed growth— a mixture of seven parts loam or good garden earth, three parts peat, and two parts sand. For seeds, all lumps, twigs and bits of fibrous matter should be removed by passing the mixture through a quarter-inch sieve. To encourage healthy, early development of the seedling's root system, add about two ounces of superphosphate to each bushel of soil mixture.

Sterilize Your Own Seedling Soil

It is quite possible to sterilize the soil you will need for seedlings right in your own kitchen without the use of harsh drenching chemicals (which are good soil sterilizers but which must only be used outdoors or where there is excellent ventilation). Small quantities of soil may be sterilized in the oven; using an old roasting pan or foil dish. (Never use a plastic flower pot for this heat process as it will melt). Set the oven temperature control at 250 to 275 degrees. Place a good oven thermometer in the center of the soil; thoroughly dampen the soil and place it in the oven until the thermometer reads 180 degrees. Remove from the oven immediately and spread the hot soil out on thick layers of paper for fast cooling.

NOTE: Do NOT use soil that has been allowed to reach a temperature of over 200 degrees. When soil is heated that high it develops a nutrient toxicity problem, and plants or seedlings will not live in such soil.

START YOUR OWN SEEDS

I've often thought that the one sure way in which the town and city gardener can triumph over an environment of tall buildings and scant sunlight is to start seeds growing. Probably more excitement and satisfaction is derived from planting a pan of seeds than any other form of in-town gardening.

When you follow all the rules and do things the right way, starting seeds is really quite a simple task. Whether you are starting your own vegetable plants or annual flowers, the same rules apply. Some of the materials may have changed over the years and so even if you are an experienced gardener there are new possibilities.

Nowadays, instead of being forced to start each variety of seed in a separate container and then having to transfer the young seedlings into a second container where they mature before finally going into the garden, there are much more simplified methods. Let's look at both ways.

Fill flats with sterile soil.

The Old-Fashioned Way

Of course there is a great deal to be said about the value of sowing seeds the old-fashioned way because it has proven successful. The planting medium is the first consideration. You can go to all the work of mixing your own seedling soil, or you can visit your nearest nursery or

Make small furrows or tiny seed holes.

Sow seeds at a depth twice their diameter.

Mark each variety.

Thin seedlings to spacing recommended on seed package.

If seedings are destined to live in flower pots, they should be transplanted when first true leaves grow.

garden center and for very little money buy enough seedling soil such as peatlite to cover all your needs. If you want to mix your own, the old reliable recipe consists of seven parts loam, three parts peat, and two parts sand. To this mixture add about two inches of superphosphate in a four-inch flower pot, or a complete fertilizer such as 5–10–15, to each bushel of soil you mix. It's smart to sift the soil through a quarter-inch sieve to remove rough and lumpy material.

Place some drainage material in the bottom of each container; use bits of broken pots, or pebbles. Fill the container with soil to about an inch from the top and then tamp the soil until it is firm, flat and level. (The bottom of an ordinary drinking glass will do as a tamper.)

Dampen the soil mixture before planting. Sow each different kind of seed in a different container. A six-inch seed pan, or a five-inch flower pot will be large enough to start all the seedlings of each variety needed for the average small garden.

Now, depending on the size of the seeds you're sowing, either shake them into tiny furrows you have lined across the surface, or scatter the seeds over the entire surface of the seed container's soil. Cover the seeds by either pushing the tiny ridges of the furrows in over them, or by lightly covering them with a thin layer of soil. Shaking the soil from an old salt shaker is an effective way to cover the seeds. You may prefer to cover the seeds with a thin layer of vermiculite, or milled peat or sphagnum moss.

The next step is to add the magic ingredient—water—to start the process of germination. Using room-temperature water either sprinkle the seeded container with a fine spray from above or sit the container in water until the surface turns dark indicating that water has percolated right up to the surface from below. You may not have to apply water again if the seedling soil contains enough humus material.

Next, place some shading and a pane of glass, or plastic (such as wrapping film) or even place a sheet of newspaper over the seeded and moistened container for the purpose of keeping the moisture around the seeds until they spring to life. As soon as germination occurs, remove the shading and coverings and place the containers of infant seedlings in a good light such as on a windowsill, or under a horticultural light fixture. The bright light will keep the young plants small and sturdy (not spindly) and they will develop a good strong root system. Keep the container moist at all times, watering in the morning so that the seedlings will not have to spend the night with a surplus of wetness at their crowns.

Damping-off disease is the worst enemy of the seedling as it cuts the stems off at or just below the surface. Good control of damping-off is obtained by dusting the surface of the soil in the container (before seeding) with a fungicide that contains captan. Mix this substance into the top inch of seedling soil. Experienced gardeners often shake a tiny bit of captan into the seed envelopes and give the seeds a coating before depositing them on the soil.

When these seedlings have grown their first "true" leaves, usually about four leaves, they need to be thinned out to the spacing recommended on the package. This is called "pricking out". From the seed pans or pots, the seedlings are moved to flats that contain the same soil mix. The seedlings live this stage of their lives growing strong and healthy until large enough to be finally transplanted into the garden or wherever they are to be grown to maturity. The plants need to be hardened off before being given the shock of the indoor-outdoor changeover.

To harden off the transplants, place them outdoors for about an hour on a dull, warm day, then bring them in again. Then gradually increase the duration of their outings until the plants become hardened enough to withstand the total change. If you have enough space available for a cold frame, this is where it will pay off.

The Modern Way To Start Your Own Seeds

This is an age of great advancements in everything and horticulture has not been overlooked. For very little expense you can buy your own seed miniature greenhouse as shown in the sketches. In these little greenhouses you sow the seeds in tiny, fibrous containers such as the peat "jiffy" pots, and others, and in these containers the seedling stays forever. When it comes time to transplant to outdoors you simply plant pot and all into the garden soil and the plant grows on without having to suffer the shock of transplanting or root disturbance.

Using the miniature greenhouses is an almost foolproof way to get your plants started from seed with nearly total success. Whether you are gardening under lights indoors, in window boxes or patio planters, or outdoors, this modern method of starting your own seeds offers great promise to the town and city gardener.

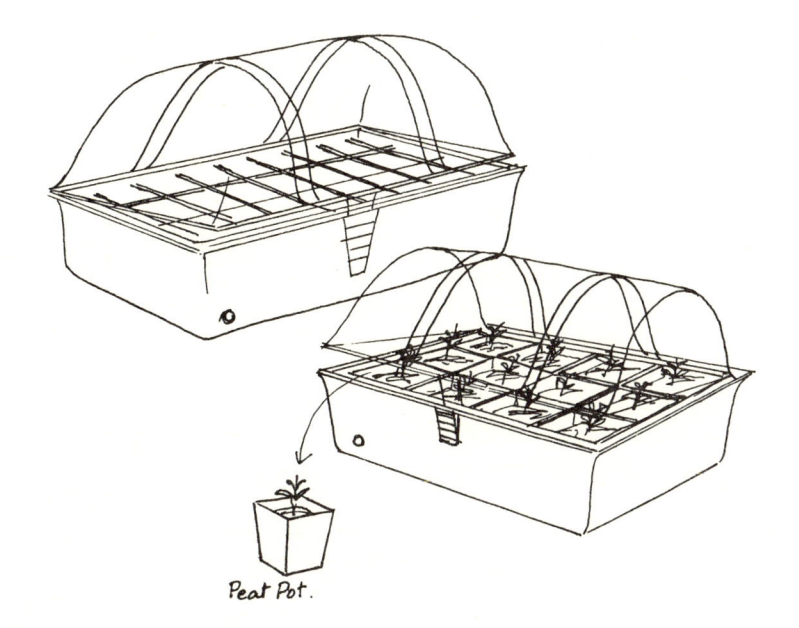

Some miniature greenhouses come with removable dividers. Others are used with peat pots. They can be used for starting seeds, rooting cuttings, growing grass plugs, and so on.

Peat Pot.

Peat pellet.

Peat pellet expanded in water.

Don't Get Started Too Soon

You will note that when you buy seeds from a reliable source, the *number of days* that elapse from time of sowing until bloom will be clearly marked on the seed package. This time is important. Obviously the seeds that take the longest time to mature will need to be started the soonest indoors.

Plants that need sixty to seventy days from seed to bloom, may be sown in a cold frame about May 1st, or in the open ground between May 10th and 15th. Plants that need eighty to ninety days from seed to bloom, may be sown indoors or in a hotbed between April 15th and 20th. Plants that need ninety to a hundred days from seed to bloom should be sown indoors or in a hotbed about April 1st—if a greenhouse is available, March 20th. Plants that need a hundred and ten or more days from seed to bloom should be sown in a greenhouse between February 20th and March 1st.

The above planting dates have been suggested for gardeners who live in a growing zone similar to that of Ottawa and who wish to have mature plants by mid-July. Gardeners living in growing zones that are milder (have more frost-free growing days) than Ottawa, could start seeds a little earlier than stated above, but the number of days from seed to bloom will remain fairly constant.

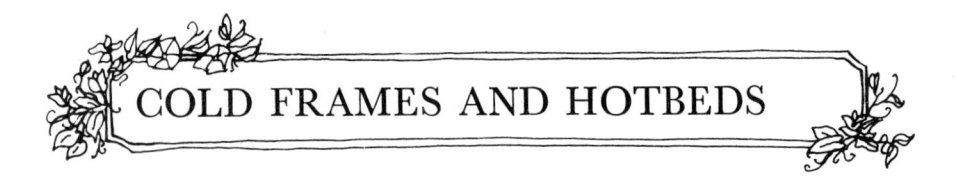

COLD FRAMES AND HOTBEDS

The whole idea of the garden cold frame is to get the jump on nature and have seedlings and transplants ready to move into the garden at the earliest possible moment after frost in the spring. The garden frame, heated or unheated, is a structure in which the gardener creates a micoclimate area that is more conducive to plant growth than the atmosphere outside it. With the garden frame, it is possible to get young seedlings into outdoor growing conditions weeks before the normal time.

When seedlings are growing quickly and require more light and space than the average home gardener can provide on a windowsill, the garden frame offers a good growing place. The cold frame relieves the space problem by allowing the earliest seedlings to be placed outdoors at least a couple of weeks ahead of time (allowing more room for the next crop of seedlings to be started indoors). The heated frame, or hotbed, enables the home gardener to get his annuals out earlier so that they do not become leggy and spindly.

Heating the Garden Frame

As its name suggests, the "cold frame" does not use any artificial heat; instead, it depends entirely on the rays of the sun and the skill of the gardener. During the bright days, the soil is supplied with heat from the sun which is retained under the glass and keeps the plants warm at night. To insulate it from outside air and to retain the sun's heat, the frame can be banked with strawy manure and covered over at night with burlap or other fibre insulating mats. As the main purpose of the cold frame is to harden-off young plants before they are placed in the garden, protection against only a few degrees of frost is necessary for about two or three weeks and so natural heat is usually sufficient.

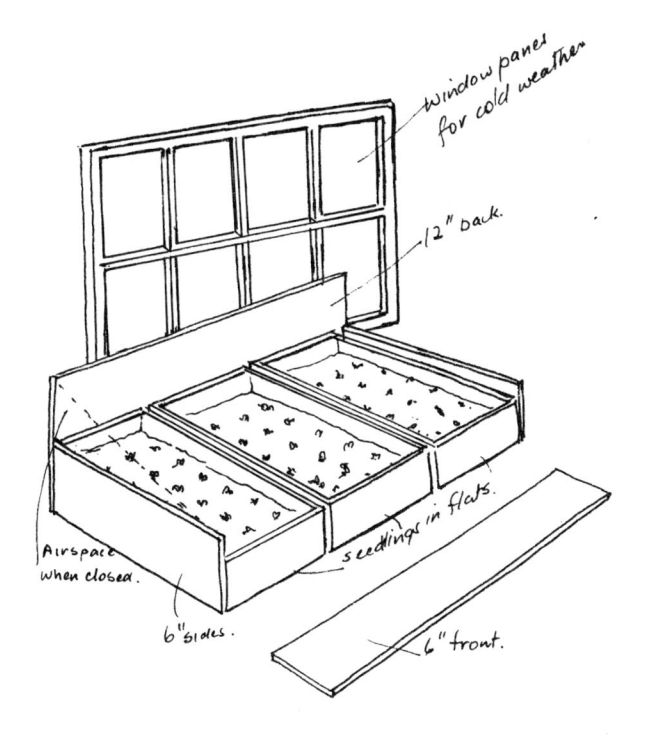

Cold frame where window sash is used.

When the proper location for the cold frame is chosen, it is possible to ward off several degrees of frost. Place the cold frame where it will receive full sun from dawn until dusk and then remember to close the frame early in the afternoon, keeping it covered with mats (as described above) until next day.

Hotbeds require artificial heating. Some gardeners have been able to locate the hotbed next to the house foundation and directly over a basement window which can be opened to allow the house's heat to penetrate the frame. Even when this is done, full exposure to sunlight is still necessary. All the normal care given hotbeds apply to this particular kind of arrangement too.

When it is not practical to construct a hotbed next to a basement window, another source of heat must be provided. This heat can come from hot water, steam, or electricity. Home gardeners have found the electric heating cable the most convenient and reliable service. Heating cables are sold in one-piece units which contain enough cable to cover the bed area of the frame. With a thermostatic control this set up can be plugged into any ordinary 110-volt house outlet.

Lay the soil-heating wire in parallel loops in the bottom of the bed. In hotbeds of two-sash size the loops can be spaced so that the cables are about seven inches apart. In a six-foot by three-foot frame the cables may be placed about four inches apart. Lay a heat-conducting material

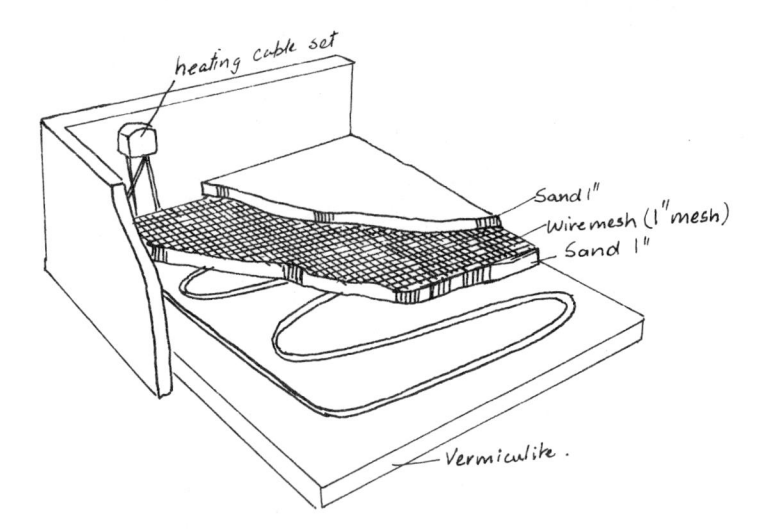

Cutaway of electrically heated hotbed

(one recommended by your supplier) directly on top of the cable, which will keep the soil temperature uniform all over the frame. When plants are to be transplanted from the flats and pots right into the hotbed's soil, six inches of good composted soil should be applied on top of the cable. If the plants will remain in the flats and pots when placed in the hotbed, the cable needs to be covered with two or three inches of sand.

Set the thermostat at about 75 degrees Fahrenheit and leave the frame closed tightly for a period of about 48 hours in order for the soil to heat up before being used. Once the plants are in the frame, window sash coverings will have to be used at night.

When the plants have been in the warmth of the hotbed for about seven days they will require some ventilation, at least on warm days. Ventilation should be done gradually. Prop the sash open with a wooden wedge or brick for only a few hours in the warmest part of the day. Be sure that the sash is closed by no later than 4:30 in the afternoon. After a few hours of ventilation daily for about seven days, remove the whole sash for the same period of time each day. When the weather becomes warm enough you can leave the sashes off all the time, but watch out for severe frosts. Water the plants in the hotbed or cold frame in the morning thus allowing the foliage the whole day to dry off.

Making the Garden Frame

Now that we've talked about where to place the frame, how to use it and what to use it for, we can now consider the size of the frame and how much money we want to invest in its construction. In researching

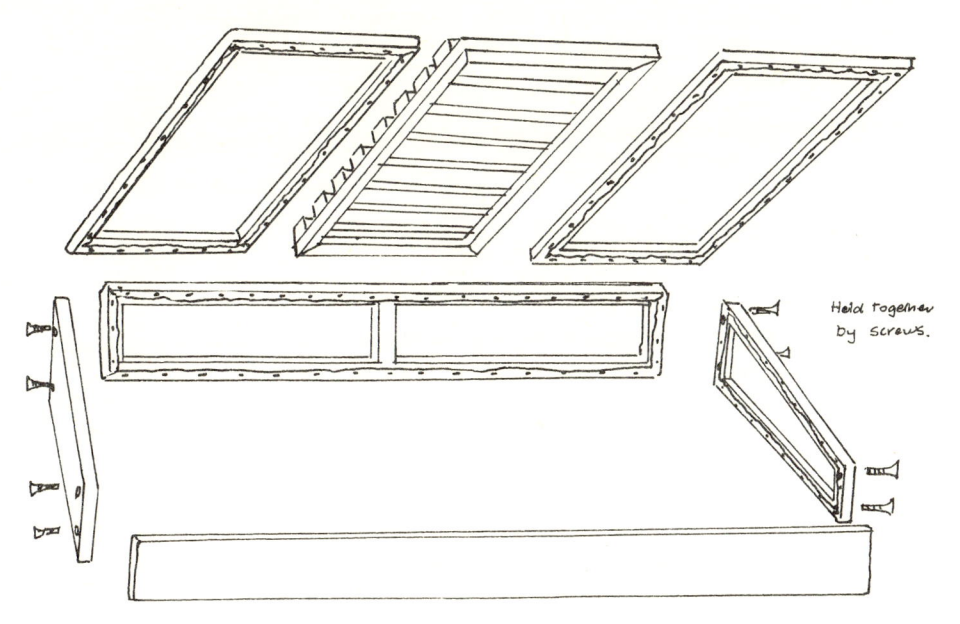

Norman Mansfield's ingenious cold frame made of 1"x2"s and polyethylene, with centre lid panel, slatted to admit air.

In gardens with limited space, a collapsible frame allows more growing room when dismantled after use.

the various construction methods and sizes, the frames used by the Canada Department of Agriculture Plant Research Institute, Ottawa, Ontario, appear to be quite acceptable.

For Those Who Have Plenty of Space

The experts at the Plant Research Institute use 6' x 3' sash or panels covered with 6 mil polyethylene plastic. (I have managed to find good, old storm window sashes at used-lumber yards and house wreckers which have been quite economical and satisfactory.) Staple the plastic to the sash and hold it in place by slats of wood nailed through the plastic to the sash so that edges of the plastic are sandwiched between. The plastic material must be replaced every year. There are longer-lasting plastics and thicker, more-rigid types but these are also more expensive. (I have kept the original glass in the used storm sash and have not needed to use the polyethylene film.)

According to the instructions received from Ottawa, the standard two-sash frame is almost six feet wide outside but can be built to any

103

length. When ordering pre-cut materials, or doing your own carpentry, here is what is required for the construction of a two-sash standard cold frame.

> 1 piece of wood 2″ x 8″ x 6′
> 1 piece of wood 2″ x 14″ x 6′
> 1 piece of wood 2″ x 2″ x 6′
> 2 pieces of wood 2″ x 6″ x 5′11″
> 2 pieces of wood 1″ x 3″ x 5′11″
> 2 pieces of wood 2″ x 8″ tapered to 2″ x 5′11″

One-inch-thick wood may be substituted for the two-inch thicknesses where the frames are going to be used only for late winter and early spring service for early vegetables and annuals, as these can be taken apart and stored after use each year.

Hardware needed for construction includes:

> 2 L-irons 2″ x 2″ x 12″
> 2 L-irons 2″ x 2″ x 6″
> 24 round-headed bolts ⅜″ by 3″ with washers
> 30 number 8 nails.

I suggest that when you next pause in your gardening activities to make plans for the future use of the space at hand that you consider all the interesting possibilities and advantages of keeping a cold frame or hotbed.

Scaled-down Frames

The dimensions given above for the cold frame may be too large for many town or city gardeners, but, there is no harm in scaling the sizes down to suit whatever space you have available. As the illustrations show, handy portable cold frames can be made in any number of ways.

Many a downtown gardener has been able to take advantage of such places as basement window wells and basement stair wells by glassing them in with some old storm sash thereby creating either a small cold frame-like area or even a compact little greenhouse.

If you don't happen to have a ground level window or a window well around which you can build your cold frame, but you do have a window that faces approximately south, you could join the thousands of town and city people who have installed small in-window greenhouses. These small greenhouses can be extremely valuable growing areas when heated by the regular home-heating system with the addition of sunlight.

Innovative apartment dwellers are designing their own balcony cold frames and greenhouses that can be taken in, folded up and stored away until needed again in the spring.

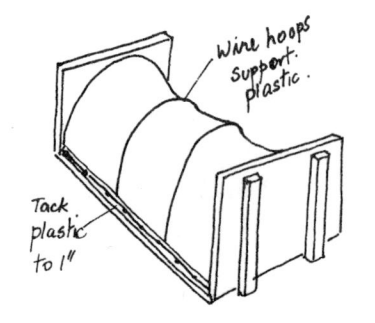

Small cold frames can be made various ways. This one uses wood, wire and plastic.

Cold frame using storm sash over window well

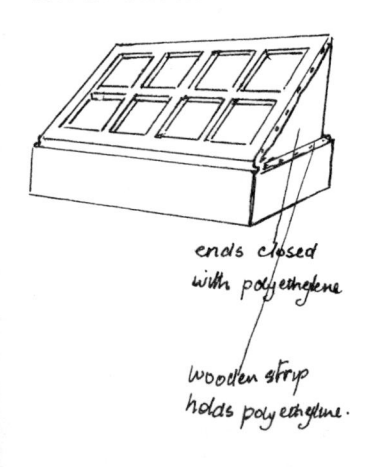

A window greenhouse is useful for starting seedlings and cuttings.

ROOTING SHRUB CUTTINGS

Only minimum space is required. Where there just isn't enough space to establish a cold frame or hotbed, there certainly won't be enough room for a standard greenhouse either, and yet it is still possible to become involved in an extremely interesting project. If you can find two square feet of space in the sunshine, you can make a propagation case and root the softwood cuttings of various shrubs and woody ornamentals. Best of all, there isn't anything easier to make and operate.

All that's required is a wooden box 4 inches deep, about 20 inches long and 15 inches wide, a sheet of clear plastic (an old dry cleaning or laundry bag will do), and three or four bits of stiff wire, or pliable bamboo rods, or maybe a willow branch to be used as supports for the plastic covering. The plastic is spread over the hoop-like supports which makes the box look like a miniature covered wagon. A box of the suggested size will easily contain up to a hundred cuttings spaced at inch intervals, in rows two inches apart. When the cuttings have been inserted, the plastic should be drawn tightly around the box and supports, locking out all air and keeping moisture in. Make provision for the spout of a watering can or the nozzle of a mister to be inserted.

Plastic over wire loops

Flap left for insertion of spray.

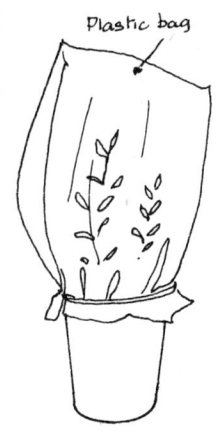

Various miniature greenhouses work as propagation cases.

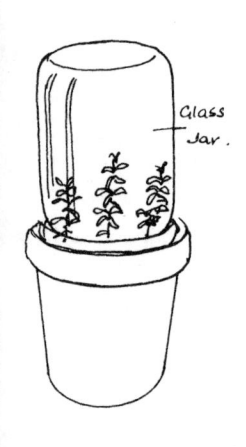

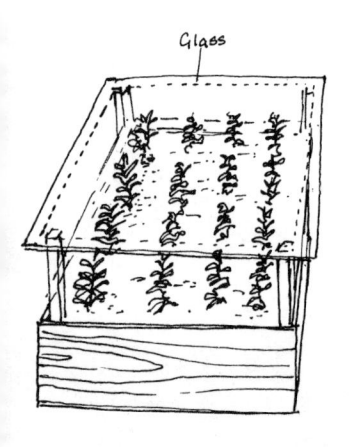

A Miniature, Miniature Propagation Case

When the home gardener has no need for a hundred rooted cuttings, he can create growing conditions similar to the plastic "covered wagon" type box which will accommodate only five or ten cuttings. The miniature greenhouse can be made by using a 6 or 7-inch flower pot filled with rooting medium. The cuttings are inserted, and then a wide-mouthed glass jar turned upside down over them. The jar acts as the plastic does on the bigger case to keep air out and hold moisture in.

When and What to Cut

Depending on your own local growing conditions and climate, the time to make softwood cuttings is about mid-June to the end of July. Cuttings of the green wood, or the current season's growth, must be used for rooting purposes; older wood will not perform.

Choose leafy stems that have been produced this year. Pick the ones that tend to snap easily. Make the cuttings oversized, about a foot long, as they can be trimmed to suitable size later.

Many of the most common hedge and shrubbery plants are among the easiest to propagate in this way, including: arctic willow, alpine currant, amur privet, spirea, highbush cranberry, mock orange, cotoneaster, honeysuckle, snowberry, variegated elder, hydrangea, forsythia, Somerset daphne, tamarix and weigela.

Some Handy Equipment

When the day comes to go out and gather your softwood cuttings from your own garden it will be worth your while to carry a pair of pruning shears, some twine or twistems, a polyethylene bag, and labels. The cuttings will stay firm and juicy for hours in the plastic bag without harm until you are ready to make the actual properly-cut cuttings. Make bundles of about ten of each kind of cutting and then tie and label them for identification.

The Rooting Medium

Softwood cuttings require a planting medium that will retain enough moisture to meet the needs of the young roots. The mixture should be one that will not become waterlogged, or hard and dense. The most acceptable mixture is equal parts of peat moss and sand. I have had success rooting softwood cuttings in a mixture of perlite, peat moss, and vermiculite in equal amounts. I find that far less damage is done to the

Keep cuttings moist.

Level the planting medium.

Dip the rooting end in hormone powder or liquid.

Seal cuttings in a container.

hair roots when removing the cutting from the box when this mixture is used. A much larger and still intact rootball stays on the cutting thus giving me far more success after transplanting.

Whichever rooting medium is used, fill the box to within half an inch from the top and then tamp it down firmly with a wooden block. The firmness acts as support for the cutting before roots grow to hold it upright.

Preparing and Planting the Cuttings

To ready the cuttings for planting, choose the semisoft tip wood and make a slanting cut just below a node, which is the point on the stem from which a leaf or leaves sprout, leaving the overall length about 8 inches. Remove the leaf from the two lowest nodes and dip the rooting end of the cutting (the thick end) in either powdered or liquid commercial rooting hormone. Be sure to purchase the right strength of growth-stimulating hormone—full directions will be found on the label.

When the cuttings have been properly prepared they should be immediately inserted in the rooting medium. Never force the cuttings by ramming them home. Make a hole with a pencil or a finger, insert the cutting and then firm them up to squeeze out all air pockets. When the box (or flower pot) is full, apply plenty of water from above in the form of a fine sprinkle or spray. After the watering comes the plastic wrapping and addition of hoop-like supports. Fasten the plastic—with tacks, pegs, staples, or whatever you choose—to the box and framework, forming the covered wagon. Be sure your wrappings will be *air tight* as they must keep air out and moisture in. At one end, allow for an opening into which the spout of a watering can or nozzle of a mister can be poked.

Place the planted and sealed container in the sunshine, but be sure to provide shading during the hottest part of the day. A cloth on a frame makes ideal shade. It is not likely that the cuttings need be disturbed, not even for watering for the first ten days, although it would be wise to make certain that the leaves are never allowed to become dry.

After 20 or 25 days you can satisfy your curiosity and pull out one of the cuttings to see whether or not roots have begun to form. Remember that some kinds of cuttings root faster than others.

When the cuttings are well rooted, plant them in a protected place in the garden and provide daily overhead sprinklings until all signs of wilt disappear. Leave them where they are until the following spring at which time they can be planted in their permanent location. If you prefer, the cuttings can be left and transplanted in the fall, allowing them one more full growing season before they are moved to their permanent home.

ROOTING HARDWOOD CUTTINGS

Nature can be put to work propagating shrubs and trees during the freezing winters too. There are many deciduous shrubs and some trees that can be propagated by means of hardwood cuttings that are taken from the time of leaf fall to as late in the winter as February, depending on the species concerned. Some of the most commonly desired plant material that is multiplied in this manner include such shrubs as: barberry, alpine currant, diervilla, dogwood, privet, forsythia, spirea, and the various mock orange. Some trees propagated by hardwood cuttings include: poplar, cherry, willow and peach.

When and What to Cut

Cuttings of about pencil-thickness should be taken from healthy wood of the current season's growth. As mentioned above, these cuttings may be taken in November or early December after the leaves have fallen. With most shrubs the entire length of the shoot (or new branch) can be used, cutting it into sections 10 to 12 inches long. Each section (or cutting) should have two or more sets of buds (also called nodes or joints).

Use a sharp knife when cutting the shoot into sections. Make a clean, diagonal cut just *above a bud at the top*, or apex end, and just *below a bud at the bottom* of each cutting. The cut at the top should always slant towards the bud. It is a good idea to make some slight difference between the cuts made at top and bottom so that the different ends can be distinguished.

Each variety should be tied in separate bundles of cuttings and fully labelled.

Rooting the Hardwood Cuttings

There are two methods of rooting the hardwood cuttings, both of which should be convenient to the city gardener with even a tiny amount of garden space in which to work. One method is to plant the cuttings directly into a specially prepared outdoor bed. Prepare enough sand and peat moss to cover the little cutting bed six inches deep. Be certain that the bed has excellent drainage, so that water will not stand and rot the cuttings. Plunge the cuttings to about two-thirds to three-quarters of their length into the mixture, and keep them well watered until the ground becomes frozen.

Some form of winter protection will be needed, such as evergreen boughs or a layer of leaves or straw. As soon as the snow melts in the spring, uncover the cuttings and allow approximately eight weeks of warm weather before discarding those cuttings that have not taken root and broken into bud. After that first summer and autumn when the leaves have dropped from the cuttings, they may then be transferred to

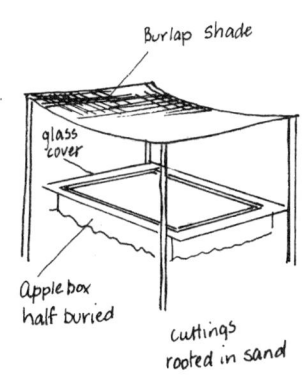

Hardwood cuttings require a winter's sleep before rooting. They can be rooted in a nursery bed or a box. Shade should be provided.

a bed consisting of garden soil, or to their permanent location.

The second method of rooting the hardwood cuttings offers the gardener a choice of two ways to store the cuttings through the winter. (a) The bundles of cuttings may be buried in slightly moist sand, peat moss, or sawdust and kept in a cool area where the temperature ranges between 40 and 45 degrees. (b) Where there is no such cool area to store the cuttings for the winter, the bundles may be buried outside in a small pit filled with peat moss and sand, or perlite (which I have used with great success) making sure that the bundles are placed below the frost line. I have also found that dipping the rooting ends of the cuttings in rooting hormone powder or liquid help greatly to start the development of sprouts.

In the spring, when the soil is workable in the garden, remove the bundles of cuttings from their storage and plant them individually in nursery rows with the bottom two-thirds of the cutting set below the ground level. Plant them on an angle so that the rooting end is no more than two or three inches below ground. Roots and leaves will soon form and you have a new supply of plants. These rooted cuttings can be moved to their permanent locations just as soon as they are of reasonable size. If transplanted while there is still active leaf growth on the cutting, be sure to provide light shading for a few days after planting, and keep the area moist for several days to help reduce uprooting shock.

FROM SEEDS TO TREES

Each time I see the seedling of a tree emerge through the soil and remember that I harvested the seed, treated it, planted it, and will some day see it standing proud and tall, I get excited. Gathering tree seeds and starting them into life is a gardening experience that everyone can enjoy no matter what their living conditions or life-style. In the section on starting softwood cuttings I state that the barest minimum of equipment is necessary to do the job. When it comes to starting trees from seeds all that is required is a four-inch flower pot, a glass jar with lid, and a bit of seedling soil. That's all.

There is a special feeling of pride and accomplishment that goes along with starting trees that is more intense and satisfying than almost any other gardening endeavour. The realization that from that tiny, almost weightless seed will grow a stately tree that in many cases will outlive all of us is indeed cause for a feeling of satisfaction. A tree is a wonderful legacy for the world.

Patience is Needed

From the time you gather the seeds until you have trees that are large enough to pass around the neighbourhood as planting-sized gifts, four to five years will elapse. The seeds of some trees such as elms can be picked from the tree when ripe and planted directly into the soil, in the same manner as vegetable seeds are sown. From these, tiny seedlings will appear in about one week. Then there are other types such as roses, hawthorns, and native holly (where it is hardy), which can also be taken directly from the plant, cleaned, and sown in the soil. These will take twenty-four months to germinate.

Seed Harvest Times

Not all trees, nor even all species of the same genus of tree produce mature seeds at the same time. For example, silver maples and red maples make their seeds available during June, while the Norway maple and sugar maple won't give up their seeds until September.

Seeds to Store or Not Store

Some seeds can tolerate storage conditions for long periods while others won't last for even a short time. The seeds of maples, elms, and oaks, for example, must either be sown directly into the soil right at the time of harvest or they can be stored over the winter in the refrigerator in sealed jars with moist sand and peat moss. (Do not store them in the freezer.) Storing the acorns of the oaks indoors for the winter is the surest way of keeping them hidden from industrious squirrels and chipmunks.

You will notice that many seeds stored in this way will begin sending out growth sprouts long before planting time in the spring. When they are planted in the soil in this condition they do not seem to be as attractive to the hungry animals. For examples of seeds that can be kept for a long time, there are the seeds of leguminous trees including the Kentucky coffee tree (*Gymnocladus*), yellowwood (*Cladrastis*), black locust (*Robinia*), and honey locust (*Gleditsia*) which can be stored for several years before being sown in the soil.

As for determining which seeds can be stored, I rely on my own observations to tell me whether or not nature would start them out right away or keep them dormant for a while. If you are not in a position to be able to keep an eye on nature's habits and you are unsure about storing certain kinds of seeds, I suggest you contact the nearest gardening authority about the matter.

Seeds Often Need Treatment

Once again I rely on my observations of how nature treats each kind of seed and then I try and emulate her ways with the seeds I have harvested. I've found that seeds often need some kind of special care before being sown.

All seeds are equipped with some sort of covering, or various appendages and devices which will help them spread themselves over the widest possible area. Birds, animals and wind are usually the carriers of the seeds.

The seeds of basswoods, for instance, are given a parachute that lifts and floats on the gentlest breeze and will travel miles and miles. The seeds of maples and elms are equipped with a wing that helps them to spread around. The witch hazel is one of the most discourteous seed distributors with its built-in ability to loudly pop open the seed husk and spit the seed with amazing speed and force. Oaks and other nut-producing trees are assisted in getting their seeds distributed and even planted in the soil by squirrels and chipmunks. The trees that produce seeds with fleshy coverings depend for distribution on their seeds being processed through the digestive systems of birds and animals and in this way carried to distant locations before reaching the soil. Some trees produce seeds with sticky hooks on their coverings which catch on the hair of animals and get carried away for many miles.

No matter what type of covering they have, each seed must somehow break out of its inner pod and make use of the soil's moisture and acids to start growing. Frosts and general weathering often break the seeds out, as does the process of passing through the digestive system of birds and animals.

Gardeners can sometimes speed up the germinating process by soaking hard-shelled seeds in water for a couple of days to soften the tough skin, or by using a small, finely-grooved file to file a small hole in one end as an opening for moisture penetration.

Before being sown, all seeds must be free of their hard shells, coat of burrs, layer of flesh, wings, parachutes, fluff, or whatever clings to them. Decay usually destroys the outer appendages but when trapped inside, the seeds will suffer the same destructive decay and be forever lost.

After observing and learning that nature helps the seeds get out of the shells and that frosts and weathering prepare the seeds for germination, we can artificially copy her procedures as closely as possible and make preparations to have the seeds available when and where we want them. When we discover that a certain variety of tree must have the action of frost before it can germinate, we sow those seeds in pots and leave them outside all winter.

Sometimes the procedure is a little more complicated. The seeds of the wayfaring tree (*Viburnum lantana*) require a more complicated process before they can be sown in the spring. Gardeners can imitate this

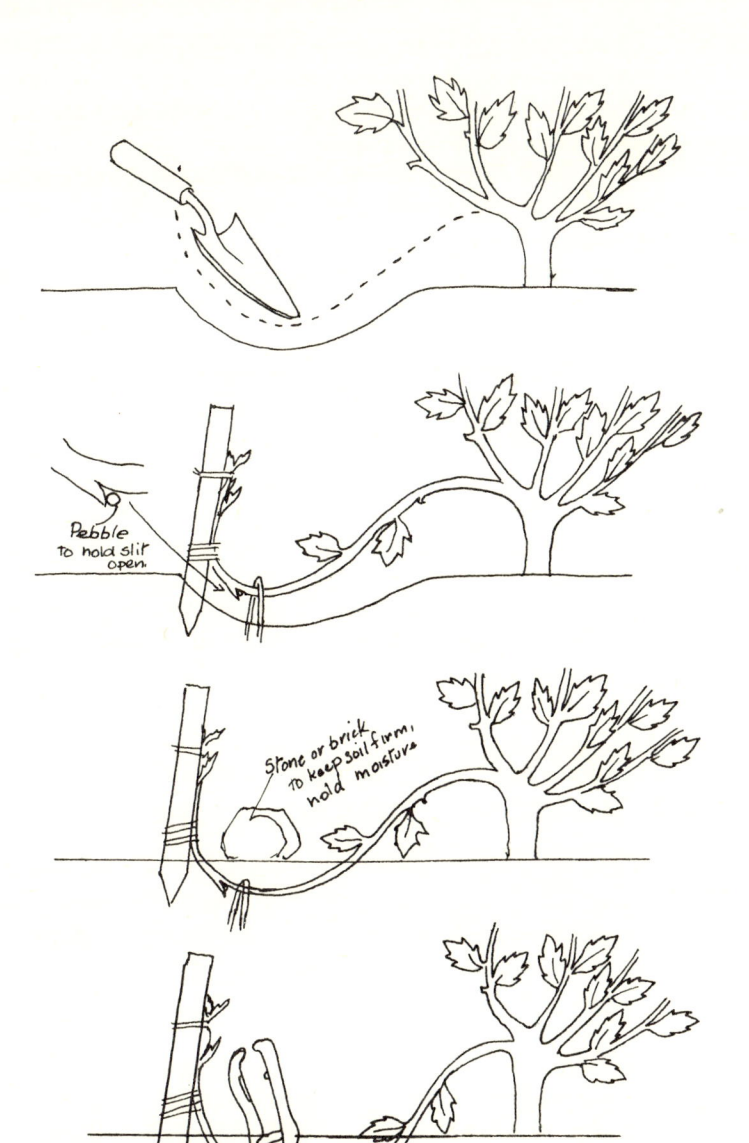

Layering is another way of rooting such plants as woody shrubs.

Pebble to hold slit open.

Stone or brick to keep soil firm, hold moisture

process artificially at home. When the wayfaring tree seeds have fully ripened and are ready to drop from the tree, gather them and mix them together with moist peat moss and sand, and store them in a glass jar (fill several jars). Keep the jars in a place where the temperature remains fairly constant at 55 to 60 degrees for the period of from 60 to 150 days (two to five months). Bring one of the jars out of the cool storage after 60 days, another after 90 days, 120 days, and then finally bring the last jar out after 150 days. In this manner you may goof on the storage time for some of the seeds, but the entire harvest will not be ruined. No matter what length of time each jar is kept in cool storage, it must then be subjected to 30 days in the refrigerator where the temperature is even cooler—about 35 to 40 degrees. After the refrigeration period, put the jar back into cool storage (55 to 60 degrees) again until spring when the seeds can be sown outdoors where they will germinate in just a few weeks.

Treatment of Seeds for Starting Specific Trees

ALDER AND BIRCH   The seeds of these trees are carried in catkins which should be gathered and placed in a sunny window and allowed to dry. Collect the seeds as they fall free of the catkins and mix them with damp sand and peat moss, put them in a jar with a tight lid. Place the jar of seeds in the refrigerator (not the freezer) for the entire winter. When spring arrives, sow the seeds in their peat-sand mixture on the top inch of pots of soil and then cover over with polyethylene film until germination. When they have germinated, remove the plastic and apply water until the seedlings are large enough to transplant.

BUCKEYES, HICKORIES, HORSE-CHESTNUTS, WALNUTS When hickory nuts have been collected they should be placed on a basement floor and left there until the tough husks crack themselves open and the seed can be easily removed. Walnuts when they turn soft and brown can be easily opened and the seed removed. Remember that the husks of walnuts produce a very stubborn stain, so you'd be wise to wear rubber gloves to protect your hands when handling their soft husks.

All the seeds in this group require the refrigerator stratification process, that is, mix them with moistened peat moss and sand, seal them in a jar, and place this container in the refrigerator. Along about February or March you will see the beginnings of small rootlets. When the rootlets appear, take the seeds from the refrigerator and plant them in small pots and set them in a sunny window until time for planting in the spring.

HEMLOCKS, FIRS, PINES, SPRUCES   Collect the cones that are the darkest brown colour and which still have tight scales. Those cones which have opened their scales have already released the seeds and are of no use to seed collectors. Dry the cones in a hot sunny location until the scales open and seeds drop out. When picked up, the dry cones will shower out seeds as though they were salt from a shaker. Clean the seeds by removing the little wings.

There are several ways to grow these conifers from seed. I will explain one method that requires the least amount of space and equipment—two usual limitations of the town and city gardener. This method is as follows: Sow the seeds in pots containing a mixture of equal parts of soil and compost or peat moss; place the pots outdoors in a garden frame, or in a sheltered location; immediately after freeze-up cover the pots with a layer of straw or leaves.

Most of these seeds will produce seedlings by early spring. You may find that some protection of the seedlings is necessary to keep them safe from hungry birds, especially robins, as birds seek out the seedlings for food. A wire mesh cage around the seedlings is good protection.

Leave the seedlings in their pots all through their first spring season, through the summer and into October. Then remove the pot from around the roots, leaving the tiny trees clumped together and transplant the clump into the garden. You may divide the clump and set each plant out individually the following September (after eleven more months).

You will be delighted and surprised at how quickly the seeds of these evergreens are transformed into shapely young trees to grace your property for many years.

EUONYMUS AND MAGNOLIAS   Gather the seeds of any of the many varieties of these trees and remove the exterior coat. Also remove the fleshy surface from the hard fruit. These seeds may either be planted directly into the garden, or given the treatment of storage in a sealed jar, having been mixed with sand and peat moss and then kept in the refrigerator for the winter.

BIRD CHERRY, CHOKECHERRY, CRAB APPLE, HACKBERRY, AND MOUNTAIN ASH   As per the instructions for all seeds, the outer coating must be removed if the seeds are to avoid decay. All these varieties produce seeds that are protected by a thick layer of pulpy fruit. This layer must be removed before planting. When the seeds are bared they should be allowed to dry for a period of about ten days. If they have been sown in pots and left outdoors all winter most of these seeds will produce seedlings during the following spring. Some may not germinate until the second spring.

A method of removing the seeds from fleshy containers such as crab apples, cherries, etc. is to place them, a few at a time, in a pail of water where you can pound them with a stick. The viable seeds will sink to the bottom while the pulp and useless seeds will remain on the surface where they can be skimmed off and discarded.

ASH, ELM, AND MAPLE   After having been cleaned, the seeds of these trees should be sown in pots just as soon as possible after they have been collected. The reason for hasty planting is that the seeds must not dry out. Place the seeded pots in a garden frame or other protected area. Right after freeze-up cover the pots with a layer of leaves or straw. Most seeds of these trees will germinate in the spring.

Results to Expect

It is not unreasonable to expect within fifteen years of the time you harvest tree seeds to see a good-sized tree; I have grown Scotch pine from seed to thirty-four feet in height in that time. Alders have been known to grow to fifty feet, and silver maples as tall as forty to forty-five feet in a similar period of time.

A word of warning—when you know that a certain tree is a cultivar, that is, the product of cross-breeding, or special breeding, (such as 'Koster' blue spruce, and 'Crimson King' maple) do not try to grow trees from their seeds. The seedling of cultivars seldom come true and will not become the classy specimens that have the characteristics of the parents.

WINTERING TREES

Bringing trees safely through the winter may require that you take certain steps. People who live in the part of the world where winter is winter, and where all life, plant and animal (including people) would almost seem to be of especially hardy stock to survive, have developed special ways of accommodating themselves to the seasons. We know that if we plant things outdoors that are not winter-hardy we can't expect them to live through the winter. We are fully aware that a frost-tender plant would perish during a winter in areas where there is even a few degrees of frost. Experience has taught us where to grow what and which plants will thrive.

For our trees the main objective is to devise winter protection. Both evergreen and deciduous trees benefit from a carefully-planned protective micro-climate in the area immediately surrounding the plant. This may be accomplished through various methods as outlined here.

Provide Protection at the Right Time

Don't start too early. Be sure that the plant has gone into its winter rest period before applying protective coverings, etc. Before the weather has turned sufficiently cold the plant will not be ready and the protection you provide may force the plant into a stage of active growth, which would then make it sensitive to serious frost damage.

Winter Tree Injuries

Winter can be hard on the trees that fall victim to frost cracks, winter sunscald, browning (as of evergreens), breakage due to the weight of heavy snow and ice, and damage by rodents and other hungry animals. Except for the weight of snow and ice on boughs and branches it is not so much the cold itself that makes for breakage as it is the alternate thawing and freezing that causes all the winter injuries. Winter browning of evergreens is caused by the needles giving off and losing moisture during sunny days when the air warms up. Although the temperature may rise, the soil remains frozen and the roots are unable to take in moisture with the result that the needles may turn slightly brown.

Evergreens may be wrapped in burlap for the winter to help reduce moisture loss. Screens of burlap or other such porous material stretched over a frame can be erected to protect your evergreens from most of the drying effects of wind and weather. Such screens should be built so that they do not touch even the tips of the evergreen branches. Some evergreens may need the protection of a piece of plywood so that heavy loads of wet snow will be kept from over-burdening and breaking the boughs. Some gardeners prefer to provide a wooden prop under those branches and boughs·that are in danger of breakage due to heavy snows. Still others find best results from gently brushing heavy snow from the trees and shrubs with a broom or stick after each snowfall. Browning of evergreens, that is the result of the loss of vital moisture through the needles, can also be prevented by using one of the plastic-base sprays which act as an antidesiccant. These sprays are especially recommended for use on the tender broad-leaved evergreens.

Another of winter's common problems is the splitting of tree trunks. When air temperatures suddenly drop below freezing, the trunks of trees (particularly saplings) may split open and, in this way, expose their inner tissues to the drying wind. This may happen when the bark and outer wood cools faster than the inner wood. The rapid cooling and contraction of the bark usually keeps the inner wood warmer so that it contracts less. Hardwoods are far more susceptible to this uneven shrinking than the needled conifers, and such species as ash, beech, elm, maple, and oak appear to suffer the most damage.

The splitting of the trunks usually takes place at night and can sometimes ring out with a loud crack on the frosty air. When the air warms during the day the cracks will sometimes close but may re-open during subsequent cold spells. These cracks offer perfect entrances for disease and insects to get into the wood, which can eventually ruin the tree. The home gardener is well advised to keep a container of premixed tree dressing handy so that such cracks can be sealed against the wind as soon as they are detected.

Openings of up to several feet in length will sometimes develop on the south sides of trees when alternate freezing and thawing occurs. This injury can be identified by the dead bark patches which peel and expose the wood. By actual measurement differences of as much as 55 degrees can occur between bark temperatures on north and south sides of tree trunks indicating that the south sides of trees suffer the violence of almost fantastic temperature changes.

Most susceptible to this type of injury, which is sometimes called "southwest injury", are thin-barked young trees. Where there is the danger of this injury happening to young trees it is wise to construct some sort of shading which will deflect the strong winter sun. Some garden experts suggest painting the trunks with a whitewash, others prefer to wrap the slender trunks with burlap or one of the commercial wrapping materials now available. Any of these procedures helps to protect young saplings from this sunscalding damage by simply providing a shading or a deflection of the sun.

Another common winter problem with young trees, particularly those which have been recently planted, is that frost may heave them partly or wholly out of the soil. The roots of heaved trees have become frozen in a clump of ice and tend to be lifted out of the soil as other layers of ice form below. As the air warms temporarily and the ice melts, the trees remain partly lifted, or heaved above the surface. Continual thawings and freezings may push the root clump even further upward. Frequently, injury or death follows this heaving action as the roots become broken, or even worse, the roots are exposed to the wind and are dried out, which breaks the first rule in the care of trees—never allow the roots of trees to become dry at any time.

Heaving of young trees can be prevented by applying a mulch around them: by covering the soil with peat moss, leaves, strawy manure, or other such material. The mulch and whatever snow stays around the tree will act together as an insulation and put an end to the alternate thawing and freezing of the soil. Remove the mulch material in early spring. Heaving is most common in heavy soils.

The one remaining winter injury problem mentioned above, while not generally considered to be as serious as the others, is the problem of animals and rodents chewing tender, young bark. Such animals as rabbits and deer will reject the bark of trees that have been coated with a thiram paint. This paint is bitter to the taste.

Mice can be discouraged from gnawing on the bark of trees, usually fruit trees, by several methods. First and most drastic—there are many poisons and poisoned traps available which are very effectvie, but which also may do harm to other creatures including pets and harmless birds if mishandled.

One method of protecting saplings from mice is to place a fine wire mesh or screening encircled around the trunk at ground level. Mice cannot chew through it. These small rodents will also be discouraged from eating your trees when their winter cover is destroyed. After each snowfall at the start of the season, tramp and hard pack the snow around the trees. This will force it to turn to ice and freeze hard enough that the mice cannot tunnel through or hide in it.

THE SALTY CITY

During the winter, the town and city gardener is forced to cope with the additional problem of road salts. Sometimes the home gardener himself is to blame for some of those large doses of harmful salt being tossed on walks and driveways in order to melt dangerous ice and snow. When little or no care is taken during the spreading of the salt, the result can be a great deal of damage that doesn't appear until mid-to-late spring when the new growth should begin.

Precautions that must be taken when spreading salt during winter include having a good aim and being certain that none of that stuff lands on your flower beds, shrub borders, hedges or lawns. Precious few are the plants that can live in salty soil, although there are some that can tolerate the city's road-salt conditions.

A Good Way to Melt Snow

Consider spreading one of the many urea fertilizers instead of salt. This will melt the ice and snow; in fact, it will prevent ice from forming, and at the same time deposit slow-release plant food over the area which can only benefit the plant life.

Where there are sections of lawn and garden that become saturated with plowed-back, salt-laden snow from the street, over which you have no control, it is wise to flush and saturate these areas with clean water in the spring. Much of the surface salt can be washed away, while more of it will be diluted and soaked deep into the soil where it will quietly leach away.

For gardeners who are forced to stand by and watch salty snow pile up on their property doing its damage to the lawns every year, new strains of salt-resistant grasses have been developed. I suggest a thorough search of the seed catalogues until you find a seed expert who can guarantee his salt-resistant strains in your area. You may discover that these new grasses are scarce and hard to buy, but keep looking until you get what you want.

You must remember that grasses grown on soils with almost unreasonable obstacles need that extra pampering from the gardener. Read the labels on the fertilizer bags and make sure that the proper feeding ingredients are applied at the right season of the year. Grasses that have to be forced in shady and salty areas will require a fertilizer with high nitrogen content to force more growth.

Don't be bashful about asking the nursery people where you buy the fertilizer to help you select the right product. Be sure in your own mind that you have bought the one that is best suited to your conditions. You will discover that most manufacturers provide helpful information in the form of charts and other printed matter to all who purchase their goods. This information is prepared for your benefit, so I strongly recommend that you read it all very carefully.

Don't neglect watering these difficult grass areas, and keep leaves or dense thatch off the surface as over the winter the turf may be easily smothered under such a tight blanket.

Weeds are not apt to be a very serious problem in grasses that are growing in shade, but disease problems could occur. Such diseases as brown patch and snow mold can be averted by applying a lawn "winterizer" and "conditioner" in late autumn or early winter, applied according to the instructions on the package.

Above all, don't be misled into thinking that grasses and gardens in shade, and salt, and other unfavourable situations will not require extra loving care—they certainly will, so be prepared to help in the fight on their behalf.

As there are precious few growing things that can tolerate the rigors of salt in the soil; before you spend money on trees, shrubs, perennial plants, grass seed, or sod, come right out and ask the experts from whom you buy whether or not it will thrive where you live.

One tree that will withstand shade and salt conditions is the beautiful and hardy Russian olive (*Elaeagnus angustifolia*). Another is the sea buckthorn (*Hippophaë rhamnoides*), which should be planted in groups of at least three so that cross-fertilization is assured.

The European mountain ash can put up with a certain amount of salt splash and spray, but can't survive in deep shade and so it must have a certain minimum of sunlight each day in order to survive. The Juneberry or shadbush (*Amelanchier*) will also tolerate some salt and shade at the same time.

These few trees and shrubs that are listed above are merely examples and should not be considered to be the only plants that will survive in the described conditions. A close check of your catalogues and plant listings will indicate others.

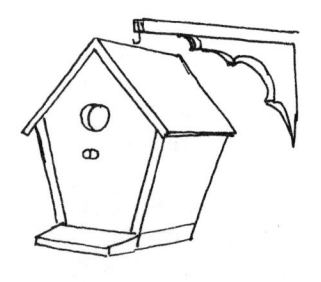

BIRDS, BERRIES & PEACE

If you have the kind of job, or live the life-style that seems to have you so sapped by the end of the day that you must have sublime relaxation, what you need is a low-maintenance garden, a retreat where wild birds come to sing and play. A bird-inviting garden is not restricted only to those who live down a country lane. Even if you have only a few square yards of open space between tall buildings you can sit and relax after a hard day and enjoy the company of birds in pleasant, calm surroundings. You will soon appreciate that the presence of birds brings a peaceful atmosphere.

Charm comes to a tiny garden with a bird bath.

Birds and Berries

Two wonderful effects are achieved if you plant berry-bearing trees and shrubs for the benefit of the birds. One of the effects is that noise is screened out. A group of shrubs act like a natural barrier to filter out unwanted sounds. When outside noises are diminished, the birds seem to sing all the more and so you reap a second benefit.

How to Attract the Birds to Deep Downtown Shade

Where you face the problem of growing trees and shrubs as bird attractions on property shaded by tall buildings, you must select shade-tolerant planting material. In your selection of shrubs, choose those which you'd like to have attract birds such as the grosbeak in the early weeks of winter. The Indian currant (*Symphoricarpos orbiculatus*), also known as coralberry, and its cousin the snowberry will be exactly right for this purpose. Several birds search for the coral berry and snowberry by instinct as these shrubs provide feed for them after the first frost.

In your shaded garden you can also grow heavy clusters of black berries in late summer by planting the vigorous, although coarse, shrub elder, the North American elder (*Sambucus canadensis*). The fruit of the American elder is such an attraction to birds that sometimes commercial orchardists and fruit-growers plant groves of these shrubs to lure birds away from their commercial crops. The red elder (*Sambucus pubens*) is very attractive and will also produce a good crop of bird fare in downtown shade.

Arrowwood (*Viburnum dentatum*) produces white flowers and black fruits which are very attractive to birds. This shrub will thrive in shade!

Grow a Hedge that will Draw Birds and Stop Noise

The following is a list of shrubs and small-to-medium trees that will produce natural feed for birds almost year round and also, when planted in combination with each other, will make a good noise-screening hedge.

Summer feed for birds can be grown on the bush honeysuckles (*Lonicera tatarica*). The birds seem to rush to the service berries and shadbush shrubs (*Amelanchiers*) when the fruit of these shrubs ripens. Over fifty species of birds flock to devour the short season of fruit on the white mulberry (*Morus alba*), a medium-sized tree.

Birds also seem to prefer the wild varieties of cherries over the cultivated types. Most popular among the wild cherries are: Black cherry (*Prunus serotina*); pin cherry (*Prunus pensylvanica*); Shubert chokecherry (*Prunus virginiana* 'Shubert'); and European bird cherry, or May Day tree (*Prunus padus*). As with most fruit trees, the wild cherries have the bonus feature of giving you attractive displays of flowers preceding the fruit.

Because the fruit clings to the tree and lasts well into the winter season, the Siberian crab apple (*Malus baccata*) is good for attracting birds and provides good blossom and foliage colours too. Almost numberless varieties of birds seek the winter fruit of the Russian olive (*Elaeagnus angustifolia*). This medium-sized tree makes an excellent screening plant and seems to be among the hardiest of all as it will grow almost anywhere.

Red osier dogwood (*Cornus stolonifera*), the gray dogwood (*Cornus racemosa*), and the pink coral dogwood (*Cornus alba* 'Siberica Pink Coral') not only produce desirable bird feed, but also make excellent screens both winter and summer with their coloured foliage in summer and their red or pink bark in winter.

Enjoy Various Colours of Plants While Feeding Birds

When planning your planting of trees and shrubs that attract wild birds, you can also be quite selective about the colours of foliage and fruit, giving your planting another dimension.

BERRIES OF YELLOW   The long lasting fruit of the European cranberry bush (*Viburnum opulus* 'Xanthocarpum') are deep-yellow, as is the produce the yellow-fruited honeysuckle (*Lonicera tatarica* 'Lutea'). Both shrubs are very hardy.

BERRIES OF BLUE   The number of shrubs that produce blue fruit is rather limited and the following is a list of the most dependable among these. Arrowwood (*Viburnum dentatum*), a relative of the highbush cranberry, is a proliferous shrub that thrives and produces fruit in almost total shade. Western blue elderberry (*Sambucus caerulea*) seems to be fairly hardy and produces powder-blue fruit. The fringe tree (*Chionanthus virginicus*), which is really a large shrub, not a tree, bears blue fruit throughout the autumn, and showy, white flowers in June. Oregon grape (*Mahonia aquifolium*) produces blue fruit among holly-like leaves. It will grow to three feet tall in either shade or sunshine. Waxy, blue fruit is borne on both Canaert and Grey Owl junipers.

BERRIES OF RED   An interesting plant to grow for red berries is the rather spectacular grape honeysuckle (*Lonicera prolifera*). This plant is actually a vine with the habit of twisting its branches into a four foot high shrub which spreads as much as six feet wide. During the summer the foliage is a silvery colour, the flowers yellow. In the fall a cluster of red, grape-like berries forms at the center of the large silvery leaves.

Some of the cotoneasters, while they have vastly different growing habits, produce red fruits that are very attractive to the birds. Diel's cotoneaster (*Cotoneaster dielsiana*) grows to four feet with arching branches and thick, silvery leaves. The Skogholm cotoneaster (*Cotoneaster dammeri* 'Skogholmen') is a ground creeper.

The inkberry, or winterberry (*Ilex verticillata*) produces holly-like fruits. Be sure to plant up to a half-dozen of this shrub as cross-pollination is needed for satisfactory berry production.

The European spindle bush (*Euonymus europaeus*) grows up to ten feet tall and bears orange seeds that are carried in vivid-red pods. Several varieties of this species also produce bright-red fruits; red cascade and 'Fructo-coccinea' among them.

Several of the viburnums also produce red fruit. Wright's viburnum (*Viburnum wrightii*) produces bright red fruit and striking crimson, autumn-coloured foliage. Canadian and European elderberries have red fruit and grow well in shade. The European and highbush cranberries (*Viburnum opulus* and *viburnum trilobum*) grow an inviting crop of red, juicy fruit.

BERRIES OF BLACK   The wayfaring tree (*Viburnum lantana*) is a large shrub that can be trained to grow on a single stem in tree-form or left to grow as a shrub. It's fruit is black and can be seen among the very early autumn-coloured leaves. Another excellent choice for black fruit is the black chokeberry (*Aronia melanocarpa*) which provides vibrant fall foliage as well as its crop of fruit. Black fruit appears on Peking cotoneaster (*Cotoneaster acutifolia*), which also puts on a spectacular show of colour in the fall. Amur privet (*Ligustrum amurense*) offers a summer of green leaves and plenty of luscious, black fruit.

BERRIES OF WHITE   The snowberry (*Symphoricarpos albus* 'Leavigatus') is likely the most popular of the white berry producers. The variety 'Mother Of Pearl' grows white berries that are tinted pink. Early summer fruit is produced on the Siberian dogwood (*Cornus alba* var. *sibirica*), and the red bark is there to be enjoyed all through the winter.

BERRIES OF ORANGE   It has sometimes been said that there are more berries than leaves produced on the sea buckthorn (*Hippophae rhamnoides*). The bright-orange berries—spectacular to see as they cluster together at the base of the needle-like leaves—attract many birds. The fire thorns (*Pyrancantha*), which are not sufficiently hardy in the more frigid areas, produce an unsurpassable crop of brilliant orange berries which are excellent fare for birds.

Berries for Birds And for People

When you have made the decision to plant the shrubs and trees that will lure wild birds to your property, you may also get the urge to grow the plants that bear fruit that you and the family can enjoy eating too. Experts have done so much work in this field that it is now possible to grow bushes that are beautifully ornamental and yet still produce edible fruit.

Currants and gooseberries are very hardy and will grow in partial shade, and they are easily cared for. The annual pruning they require keeps them in perfect shape for the small, city garden. Flowering currants have a heavy crop of yellow flowers in spring, edible berries in summer and charming, red fall foliage. The white, red and black currants are not as pretty when in flower, but turn out a much better fruit crop. The new thornless gooseberries, and the traditional thorny types, are attractive and very productive.

If you can remember when Mom, or Grandma used to bake Morello cherry pies, you'll also remember that delightful, tart flavour of the fruit. This flavour is found again in the fruit of the Mongolian bush cherry. The Nanking bush cherry also produces an edible fruit and, as with the Mongolian, is a useful ornamental bush-form cherry tree, of a size that is suitable to the small garden.

The are several other trees and shrubs that produce edible fruit and which are also quite decorative in the home garden. Check the planting lists for further species to purchase.

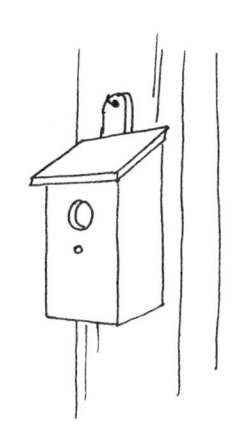

Birds will often nest in nest boxes. Each species prefers a certain hole size and height above the ground.

Winter Bird-feeding Stations

If the growing of fruit-bearing trees and shrubs has brought several species of wild birds to your garden, you may also consider trying to keep them with you all winter. It is not likely that enough shrubs can be grown to sustain a flock of birds with natural feed in the small downtown garden and so you might set up a bird feeding station. These feeding stations are available in such a vast variety of makes and design that I'll leave the choice of model to you, but I implore you to read and understand the following statement.

When you have enticed birds to remain in your garden all winter by offering them daily feedings from a safe feeding station (where cats and squirrels won't be a problem), you must NEVER neglect to have feed available to them at ALL times. The birds that choose not to migrate south and remain with you, will come to DEPEND ON YOU ENTIRELY for their winter's supply of feed. If for any reason you skip even one day of providing a supply of feed, the chances are the birds will die. Birds must maintain a constant body temperature or suffer death by freezing. In order to maintain this temperature they must have

This type of feeding station will hold enough food to last for some time.

DAILY amounts of heat-producing foods, food which cannot be found under the ice and snow (which is why birds fly south).

It would be a better and kinder act on your part not to establish a bird feeder if you plan to take a winter vacation, or leave town for even a few days. Where there is a dependable neighbour who will assume the responsibility of keeping the feeding station well supplied in your absence there is no problem. Once again, if you are doubtful that there will not be feed always available to the wild birds do not establish a feeding station or you will be luring birds to their deaths. If you do decide to go ahead with the feeding station, buy two packs of feed and keep one always in reserve against the day when you run out and cannot get to a supplier to buy a fresh supply.

TINY TREES AND SHRUBS

Getting enough variety in the small garden takes planning. Obviously one of the very real problems of setting out a garden in a small space so that it has enough variety of permanent plant life to avoid monotony, is selecting the right size of plants. When only dwarf-sized trees and shrubs are chosen, it becomes much easier to plot a garden with plenty of variety in tiny places. These days there is such a wide choice of dwarf, woody ornamentals that it is quite possible to plan a shrub garden without using any of the coniferous evergreens (which were the only choice in earlier days).

When we deal with the downtown garden or with the densely populated areas of the suburbs, we must always consider what will grow in the shade, or in places where very little sunshine penetrates. Shrubs that grow in the shade may still require lots of light; while it need not be direct, overhead sunlight, sun in the early morning or late evening may be necessary. Where an almost-sunless condition exists, the broadleaved evergreens with wintering foliage will likely be the most satisfactory.

Dwarf Shrubs for Shady Places

Those who have gardens in areas where a relatively milder northern climate prevails have a wider choice among broadleaved evergreens to plant in the shade including: the low-growing St. John's wort and its two cultivars 'Sungold' and 'Hidcote'. Salal, with its white June flowers followed by purple fruit, is another good choice. Both Aucuba *japonica* and its variegated form seem to thrive in even the deepest shade in the milder zones.

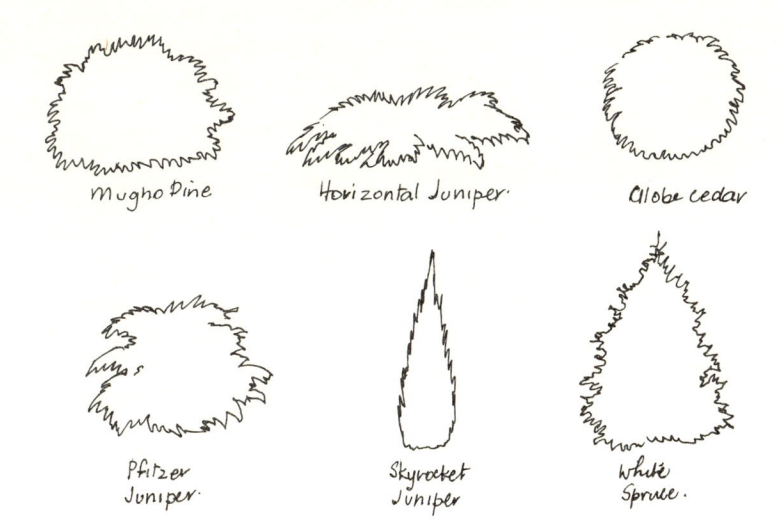

The basic shapes of evergreen shrubs

Gardeners who do not enjoy the so-called "mild" winters have a much more limited choice of broadleaved evergreens which they can grow in shaded places. One of the most delicate-looking of these is the *Pachistima canbyi* which is a low-growing plant with dark-green leaves that forms a rounded, dense shrub of about eighteen inches in height. The glossy, holly-like foliage of the popular Oregon grape is another favourite for similar weather conditions, as it bears yellow flowers in spring and fruit in summer.

Although they are not woody ornamentals and cannot be considered shrubs, two more plants that keep their broad, green leaves through the winter and which grow in shade include: periwinkle—a ground cover with evergreen leaves, blue flowers and a spreading habit; and Japanese spurge, which forms a green matting about ten inches high.

Other shrubs that have dwarf cultivars and which thrive in shaded places include *Euonymus fortunei* and its cultivars, and the *mezereon* shrubs with both rose-pink and white cultivars.

Dwarf Shrubs for Sandy Places

Those gardeners who are forced to work with dry, sandy soil also have a wide choice of woody ornamentals in dwarf form which thrive in this condition. Among these are: globe caragana, or dwarf *Caragana*; the dwarf lead plant; golden carpet broom, and spike broom; and the double dyer's greenweed.

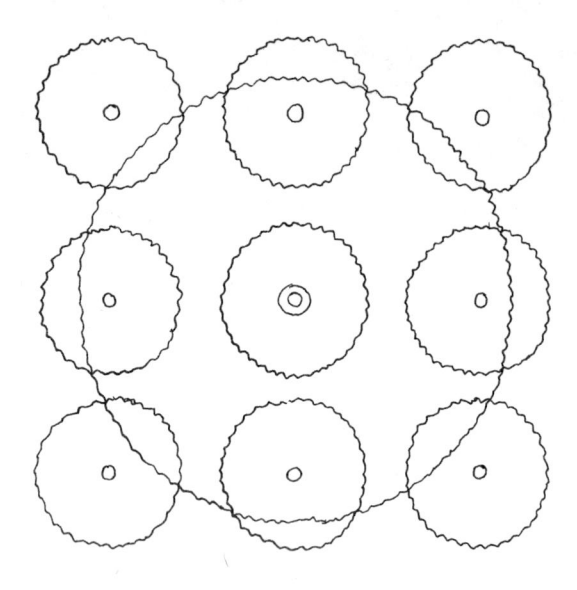

Nine dwarf apple trees will occupy the same growing space as one standard-sized apple tree.

Dwarf Shrubs for Normal Conditions

Where we do not have to consider shade or sandy conditions, the selection of dwarf-form, woody, ornamental shrubs and trees is much broader, including: two mock orange varieties, 'Frosty Morn' and 'Silver Showers'; the dwarf, red osier dogwood; the dwarf Lemoine deutzia; dwarf forms of spirea; goldrop potentilla, also known as Farrer's Bush Cinquefoil; dwarf golden ninebark; dwarf, golden mock orange; dwarf viburnum; dwarf Korean spice; and the dwarf forms of flowering almond in both pink and white.

The planting lists will indicate many other dwarf-form shrubs for planting in large variety in small garden space. Remember that here we have excluded the long list of cone-bearing (coniferous) evergreens that are available in dwarf sizes.

The Versatile Dwarfs

One of the extra charms of the little dwarf-sized trees and shrubs is that they will fit into places where plants of larger size wouldn't survive, or where larger trees would soon outgrow the space and have to be removed. In the space that would be required for one standard-sized apple tree, it is entirely possible to grow nine dwarf apple trees. Dwarf-sized, fruit-bearing trees give gardeners with limited space the opportunity to try their hand at growing a crop of fresh fruit while enjoying the added benefit of spring blossoms and brilliant, fall leaf colours.

Another example, of dwarf plants taking the place of their standard-sized cousins and doing better service in the small garden, is dwarf lilacs. These little plants grow to perfect shape and mature at about eighteen inches high and never grow any taller; they will produce fragrant clusters of flowers that are just as large as those on the full-sized plants.

Little trees and bushes also give the gardener with cramped quarters the chance to be a landscape designer on a miniature scale. Often dismal and shady little corners can be transformed into pleasantly-fragrant, pint-sized evergreen glens. Perhaps the best feature of all regarding dwarf-sized trees and shrubs is that they will thrive in a container for years. These container-held trees and shrubs can be moved from place to place to totally remove the monotony of the "same old landscape" all the time. In containers the little plants can be placed individually one on each step, leading up to your doorway. They can line your deck, patio, terrace, balcony, or downtown courtyard.

When planting little, small-scale trees and shrubs directly into the soil remember that they will look better when they are planted in groups rather than individually. You can vary the setting by planting a group of globe-shaped evergreen plants close to a group of, say, pyramid-shaped plants. Try mixing a cluster of small evergreens intermingled with a cluster of small woody ornamentals. If you mix small, spreading evergreens with small, spreading deciduous plants then in winter you get the framework of the leafless twigs mixed with the evergreen boughs for quite a pleasing effect in a very tiny downtown corner.

What is a Dwarf Plant?

Large plant species often have varieties that are small in stature. These dwarfs come about either as seedling variations or as bud mutations. Natural dwarfs are of low stature because of the creeping nature or the pendant habit of their branches. Others are simply so compact of form, with branches occurring at such very short intervals on the stalk that they cannot ever reach the full size and spread of the species from which they are derived. Remember that these are natural dwarf plants, not to be confused with cultured dwarf or the fantastically small bonsai. Trees and shrubs that have been given the bonsai treatment have been subjected to the special Japanese technique of root or shoot pruning.

Smallest and Hardiest Evergreens

Here I will list only those dwarf evergreens that are known to be hardy enough to thrive on the frigid Canadian prairies. Dwarf evergreens with this kind of stamina are certainly hardy enough to be considered perfectly safe to use in the downtown landscaping of towns and cities where the very worst weather conditions prevail.

THE PINES Low and slow-growing pine varieties which have a high ornamental value are available in large numbers. The mugho pine, sometimes called Swiss mountain pine, is an extremely slow-grower having multiple, knee-shaped, upright stems, with green to bluish-green foliage. Two of the dwarf garden forms include the cultivars Mughus and Pumilio.

Dwarf Scotch pine is very hardy and densely branched in a dwarf stature. Check plant lists for many other dwarf varieties.

THE SPRUCES The normal height for spruces can be right up to a hundred feet while some of the mounded dwarf varieties are only a few inches in height. Many dwarf species are derived from Norway spruce. These are dwarf, densely-branched, slow-growing, spreading plants in colours of light green, deep green, or bluish green. They come in both flat and round shapes. The slowest-growing spruce cultivars include Nest spruce, Maxwell, and Gregorian spruce. The Ohlendorf's spruce is broad and conically shaped. The most outstanding cultivar of the Colorado dwarf spruces is the Montgomery, which features long, stiff, bluish-green needles, a broad, conical shape and compact growth.

THE JUNIPERS The leaves of junipers are of two kinds: One is sharp-pointed and fine, the other is scale-like and flat. The leaves are green to bluish-green in summer and turn grayish-green to purple in winter. The young leaves of some varieties are a golden-yellow colour. Junipers are usually dwarf creeping plants, but there are also some that have a pyramidal or a globe shape. There are many cultivated species and cultivars, only the *hardiest* of which are listed below:

Chinese junipers—Sargent, Pfitzers's Golden, and Pfitzers's Savin junipers. The two hardiest dwarfs include Scandia and Arcadia.

Creeping junipers with green foliage—Prince of Wales and Andorra with blue foliage—Dunvegan Blue and Waukegan.

Common junipers—the golden-tipped form, Golden Oldfield, is very hardy.

THE ARBORVITAE The Arborvitae (often mistakenly called cedars) form fan-shaped branchlets that are completely covered with overlapping pairs of scale-like leaves. While the foliage is most often green, some plants have golden yellow, or silvery leaves when young. The plants are mostly upright, pyramidal or globe shaped. Hardiest of the arborvitae is the eastern white cedar.

The best dwarf-formed arborvitae are Midget and Little Gem. The best globe-shaped are Blobosa, Wareana, and Winona.

Soil for Dwarf Conifers

Most conifers prefer an acid soil where the *pH* of the soil does not exceed 6. The soil structure matters very little as long as there is good drainage and the plants don't have to stand with wet feet. Take special care to be certain that the roots are not damaged or dried out at the time of planting. Water your transplanted evergreens thoroughly every day for several days.

CRAB TREES

The novice gardener is sometimes surprised by the names and words that make up the contemporary jargon of the experienced home gardeners. A good example is the shortening of the word crabapple to just plain "crab". You'll hear nurserymen refer to their acres of "crabs", while gardeners talk about the "crab" on the front lawn or in the back garden. Although dubbed with this uncomplimentary nickname, the crab apple is in fact among the most attractive home garden specimen trees. These show-off plants will grow satisfactorily in any reasonably-good garden soil. Crabs require very little pruning, and except for an occasional spraying to prevent caterpillars early in the season, they require little or no care.

Today's market offers a choice of far more than a hundred varieties of crab apple trees. So many kinds makes it somewhat difficult to choose the varieties that are most likely to best suit your property. At mature height, a crab apple tree ranges from only six to eight feet high (ideal for the downtown garden) through to larger specimens thirty-five feet high. The best plan is to make sure that your nursery supplier knows where you want to plant your crab apple tree and helps you make a careful choice.

Largest Crab Apples

Tallest and most handsome of all the crab apples is the stately thirty to thirty-five-foot high Siberian crab apple (*Malus baccata*). This beautiful specimen features a fantastic show of white flowers in spring which precede a crop of small yellow and orange fruit. The apples of this tree are sought by birds that may come and sing in your garden. In the autumn the foliage becomes a conversation piece, and during the winter the skeleton of the leafless tree is extremely handsome in a setting of snow. Among the various varieties of the Siberian crab apple is an upright form which grows in a narrow, columnar shape of not more than six or eight feet wide. It gives you all the colour and fruiting features of the species.

Smallest Crab Apples

In contrast to the large varieties, the smallest of the crab apple family is the Sargent's crab apple (*Malus sargentii*). This one seems to be perfect for small gardens. It has a typical tree shape, growing from a single stem to a maximum of eight feet high and about ten feet wide. The flowers of this variety are usually white, although there is a form that produces rose-coloured flowers. The fruits are a striking orange.

Weeping Crab Apples

There are also very beautiful crab apple trees in weeping form with pendulous branches similar to those of the weeping willow. When these drooping boughs are laden with blossoms in the spring there is not a more striking picture anywhere in the world. One such a variety is the Red Jade, which not only features the hanging branches, but also displays a spectacular show of fruit in the fall.

Hardiest Crab Apples

Hardiest of the crab apples are the Rosybloom types. They have purple-tinted foliage and rosy blossoms. Choosing the best of the Rosybloom varieties is often difficult as some of them produce blooms only during alternate years. Where hardiness is a factor, the Rosybloom crab apples are likely the wisest choice.

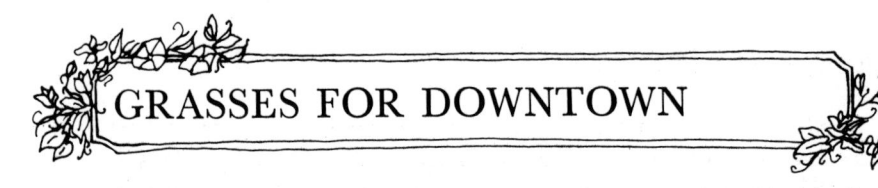

GRASSES FOR DOWNTOWN

At one time it seemed so much easier to establish a lawn and get excellent results every time. It didn't seem to matter whether we put in a small patch of green at the back of a porch in the few feet available in front of a board fence, or whether we seeded a long stretch of open, sunlit ground—grass was grass and it always grew.

Nowadays it is quite a different matter. It is no longer practical to sow just any old seed, or lay just any old sod: just ask your local greenskeepers or parks people. Air pollution in industrialized cities (which is to say all cities) is showing its effect even on our turf grasses. We must now choose grasses which are known to have a certain resistance to polluting forces.

Among the most commonly planted turf grasses are Kentucky bluegrass, creeping red fescue, creeping bent grass, and perennial ryegrass. These varieties have been given the most attention by researchers testing them for resistance to pollution. High concentrations of ozone, (a gas harmless at low concentrations, but an irritating pollutant in the high concentrations of urban industrial areas) are forced onto the surface of these grasses in measured amounts and for varying lengths of time. By measuring the effects of the ozone gas on individual grass species at different levels of development, each variety has been rated as to its resistance to injury.

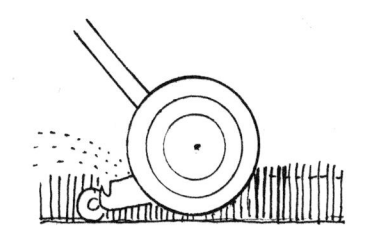

Clippings add organic matter.

Correct mowing is important. The grass should be cut before the tips bend over. Most types of grass should be cut to a height of no less than 1½ to 2 inches. Cutting too close will weaken the grass, making it go brown in the summer and encouraging weeds.

Creeping Red Fescue Resists Pollution Best

Creeping red fescue seems to be the most resistant variety of turf grass, likely because of its highly-compressed, almost drought-resistant qualities. This grass does not let water escape easily and, therefore, doesn't allow much room for particles of pollution to get into its tissues.

Armed with this research knowledge it seems that the home gardener, or sod farmer, landscape architect, nurseryman, greenskeeper and parks superintendent would all be wise to choose a grass seed mixture with a high content of pollution-resistant creeping red fescue.

Based on the available research information perennial ryegrass appears to be quite susceptible. After only one ozone treatment perennial ryegrass developed a shorter, narrower leaf.

Seeding New Lawns

For best results with a new lawn, sow the grass seed about September 1st, (unless your own local climate dictates another date; local experts will have the proper planting date available). When sown on or about September 1st, the long period of warm days and cool nights that follows offers grass seedlings ideal conditions in which to become established before winter.

The first essential requirement is good soil. Mix 20% superphosphate into the soil at the rate of twenty-five pounds per thousand square feet, (or two and a half pounds for every ten square feet of area). Next,

Spread fertilizer with an adjustable mechanical spreader.

where possible, a minimum of four inches of topsoil should be added to the soil that has been treated with superphosphate. Whether you are seeding or sodding the lawn it will root better and last longer on a good, rich base.

Make sure the variety of grass selected is suitable for your area, keeping an eye on the possible pollution problems of the district. Also get seed or sod that is suited to your shade situation and the amount of foot traffic you expect.

The seed must be evenly spread and I suggest the use of a mechanical seeder for larger areas. Sowing the grass seed by hand on small plots is quite acceptable. For hand seeding, divide the seed and sow fifty percent of the total seed in one direction and then the other fifty percent at right angles to the first spreading. Afterwards, either apply screened topsoil or rake the soil lightly by pulling the rake in one direction only to cover the seed. Raking in one direction will give you evenly spread seed and an evenly green lawn. (When the rake is pulled and pushed back and forth the seeds will pile up in neat, little straight lines and when the seeds sprout into grass the lawn will appear formed in little straight rows which is exactly what you don't want.) Water with a fine spray to keep the seedbed moist until the grass seed germinates.

Mulching the seeded surface with straw, peat moss or burlap sheets will help to hold in the moisture and cut down on evaporation. The mulch materials, peat moss, and straw, can be allowed to remain on the lawn. (Try to get chopped straw so that the stems are not too long.) This

Move lawn sprinkler only after 1 inch of water accumulates in can.

Coffee Can   Move sprinkler when 1" of water in can.

134

mulch will decompose naturally and add to the humus content and enrich your soil. The burlap sheets can be removed before the seedlings begin to pierce through the material.

The purpose of any covering is to help the ground retain moisture until germination occurs after which time they are not required. If the burlap sheets are left on the seedbed (which is quite often the case) the cloth will eventually rot and disappear. The burlap is porous and fibrous enough to allow the young grass seedlings to grow through without difficulty. In such hard-to-manage places as slopes and hillsides, it is an excellent idea to leave the burlap in place in order to help stop soil erosion while grass is becoming established.

CHILDREN'S GARDENS

Count the kids in too. Based on personal experience, I can assure you that when the children are given an opportunity to do things on their own they take an interest in the garden that you never would have guessed was possible.

Let them buy their own seed, with your supervision, and give them a little patch of ground to work and the children will surprise you with the intensity of their interest. Since this interest is sometimes short-lived try to steer them to the sunflower, bean, corn, and zinnia seeds—all plants which germinate in a fairly short time and yield quick, satisfying results.

It may become obvious that the kids aren't really all that zealous about gardening, but rather that they are thrilled to be doing the same things they see their parents doing to make things grow and thrive. Don't expect them to knuckle down and devote themselves to their garden for any great length of time; however, a variety of little jobs, in addition to the care of their own personal garden patch, may keep them interested.

Make sure that the soil you have allotted to your beginning gardener is rich and workable and that it has lots of sunshine. Remember, a satisfying experience with good, quick results will get children (and grown-ups too) off to a good start. And get them their own tools, not toys, but real and sturdy small-size garden tools.

Either help them, or at least show them how, to work up the little plot you've assigned, and be sure to be there for the application of fertilizer. After that leave them on their own to plant and water their plot. It won't matter whether the rows are straight or as crooked as a dog's hind leg; let them do it on their own. You may find that tiny tots, even six years of age will be able to mark off rows and get the seeds

The magic of a bean sprouting in a glass

into the trenches. When fast-growers are used, such as radishes, pumpkins, and others mentioned earlier, especially those that produce big seedlings, the amount of interest naturally increases. The children will be anxious to keep them well-watered and weeded. When the seedlings have sprouted up a few inches, teach the children how to apply a mulch of peat moss which will keep weeds down and hold moisture in. The children should also be taught about thinning out the seedlings and about transplanting, as the seeds will no doubt have been sown too thickly.

They will really enjoy providing shading for the transplants. Let them use their imagination for finding suitable shading materials. Just show them what must be done to keep the strong rays of the sun off young transplants until the little shoots have hardened off and can withstand the heat, by providing shade with shingles or paper hats, or cardboard shields, etc.

If you do not have enough space to spare for a children's garden, smaller children will often enjoy a flower pot garden. Give them a few flower pots which they can fill with soil and in which they can plant seeds. When such seeds as peas, beans, pumpkin, and others of large size are used, the kids can fill, dump out, seed and reseed, over and over again, and despite this rough treatment some seeds will manage to survive and germinate and thereby give the youngsters some early knowledge of making things grow.

I do not claim that all your children will turn out to be expert horticulturists or that they will carry a life-long eagerness for gardening. I do suggest that when they are allowed to start young enough, children will have some knowledge and insight of how things grow so that when they are older (teenagers) they can be of real help around the garden. One very important by-product, of your investment of time and interest in their gardening efforts, will be a degree of respect shown for lawns and gardens that they might not otherwise have learned.

Indoor Projects for Children

For the town or city dweller who does not have the luxury of even a small plot of land to turn over to the kids, there are still things that you can give them to plant and watch grow.

Supply your young children with a small bottle filled to about two-thirds with soil. Have them poke some dried beans (or bean seeds) into the soil against the glass, then apply moisture. Have them keep the soil moist and in a surprisingly short time they will be able to watch the beans burst open, send down roots and send up stems towards the surface.

If you don't think the bean bottle will work for your youngsters, make them a small pad of a half-dozen thicknesses of paper towel laid flat with some aluminum foil on the outside to retain moisture. Dampen the paper and lift the top two layers and sprinkle on some flower seeds, then replace the top layers. Have the children lift up the flap for a few seconds every day and peek at their seeds. They'll be in for a pleasant surprise when they see the seeds begin to germinate between the sheets of moist paper.

Give them a flower pot partially filled with soil and also give them a single tomato plant (or a few tomato seeds). Let them apply water and keep the pot in a bright, warm place. With continual watering they can grow their own tomatoes.

A fascinating winter project for the kids is planting and growing flowering bulbs in pots of soil. Be sure to buy only those bulbs that are are ready for indoor forcing, then follow the directions on the pamphlet that will come with the bulbs.

You will certainly find it well worth the money if you present your child with the right sized pot of soil and an amaryllis bulb. Your children will be amazed when they see those gigantic flowers open and bloom. Just be sure that their pots of bulbs are never given too much heat. Sixty-five degrees F. should be the maximum temperature for good results. There are dozens of garden projects to interest children indoors and out if Mom and Dad lead in the discovery.

VEGETABLE GARDENS

An ingenious strawberry barrel needs only minimum space.

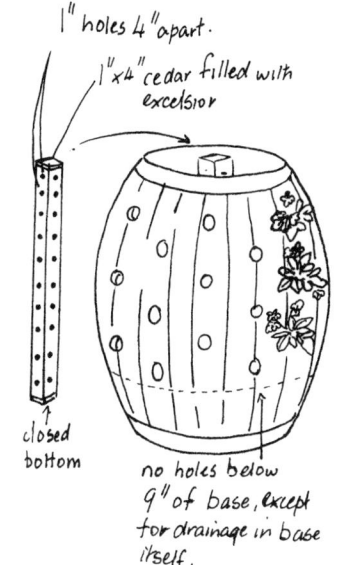

Nothing tastes as delicious as freshly picked vegetables from your own garden—juicy, full of goodness. Vegetables grown in window boxes, patio planters, and under light fixtures have been discussed elsewhere in this books. (When people want to grow vegetables they will find a place to grow them). This section here will deal with the growing of vegetables in a broader and more complete way.

The economic and environmental climate of the Seventies has brought about an interest in home-grown food that has never been seen before. Companies that supply seed are finding themselves hard-pressed to keep up with the overwhelming demand.

All would be well indeed if everyone had enough gardening space on which to grow fresh vegetables but where the gardener in a crowded, densely-populated location has even a few square feet of earth that can be devoted to growing vegetables, he or she can, with planning, grow a surprising volume of fresh food.

First Things First: Sun, Rain, Protection

Will your vegetable patch get four to six hours of sunlight per day? It should be exposed to full sunlight during most of the day in order to keep the above-ground growth lush, and vigorous. Given too little sunlight, vegetable plants tend to become spindly and leggy and do not produce a good yield.

Will it be possible for you to provide water when there is a shortage of rain? Vegetables are relatively fast-growing plants that require constant moisture in their diet. Tomato plants, for example, should never be allowed to become completely dry; alternate spells of wet and dry often cause brown rot on the fruit.

Can the vegetable patch be protected from the traffic of people and animals? A major consideration in towns and cities is whether a garden will survive the pilfering and snitching of mischievous people, to say nothing of the trampling that might be caused by careless feet or the severe damage that might be inflicted by stray dogs and cats.

The Soil

The most important consideration of all is the soil in which the vegetables are to be planted. In many areas the soil that town and city dwellers must work with is hard and dry. Often the gardener has only the almost-useless subsoil that was dug out and left on top when the basement was excavated. Substrata soils are often shale, hard clay, or dense, fine sand, none of which can support life satisfactorily.

With hard work and some soil conditioners this *subsoil can be improved* and reconditioned to the point where it can be used as a growing medium. The first chore is to spade down eight to ten inches and remove all rocks, roots, and other debris: in general, loosening up the whole area. If the earth is a hard clay or very fine sand, some drainage material will have to be placed about a foot under the surface. In order to do this, the entire surface area must be lifted off while about an inch of gravel or coarse building sand is spread over the area. This will allow excess water to seep away from the plant roots and prevent rot damage to the roots.

After you have attended to the drainage, you must then look to the water-retaining capacity of the soil that you have excavated from the bed. Vegetables need a loose, friable soil. Such soil will contain sufficient organic matter (humus) to hold moisture for the plant's needs but still allow excess water to seep away. This means mixing into your subsoil material generous quantities of sharp, coarse building sand, combined with well-rotted manure, or peat moss, or, if available, garden compost. It would not be out of line to mix in as much as half a bushel of humus to each bushel of subsoil.

Try to bring your growing medium to such a consistency that you can poke in your hand or a stick with ease to a depth of about a foot. Without enough organic matter in the soil it will remain hard and dry and quite unsuitable for vegetable growth. Root crops such as carrots, radishes, beets will be stunted and misshapen when they are forced to struggle in hard, dry earth. Moist and loose soil allows roots to penetrate deep and wide and to grow to normal maturity.

There are also man-made soil conditioners that do a good job. Look for baked clay pellets, or perlite, or vermiculite. All these materials can be worked into the soil to help improve its structure.

The Easy Method

If you want to do all the hard work described above to rejuvenate and recondition the soil that is there, more power to you. However, it would be so much easier to simply loosen the surface of the existing soil by spading or forking it up, and then covering it with about six to nine inches of good topsoil. Before you apply the topsoil, spread an inch or two of gravel or sharp sand over the area to improve drainage. A retaining wall to hold the topsoil in place can be formed by placing an eight-inch plank on edge. This will keep the topsoil from washing away or from being flattened under foot. All the work done up to this point has been to provide the plants with an anchorage, something in which they can stand and grow.

Nutrition in the Soil is Essential

When the vegetable bed is structurally ready, whether it is built with fresh topsoil, or the existing subsoil has been improved, the next step is to provide plant food. Vegetables need this in order to thrive.

Natural plant foods in the form of well-rotted manure or composted manure are good, and should go into the soil. None of these can be considered to be a complete fertilizer. Remember that well-rotted manure is an excellent soil conditioner with some plant food value, but with not enough to sustain vegetable growth in difficult growing conditions. In order to fill the heavy nourishment needs of vegetables, a commercial fertilizer must be applied following the instructions on the bag. Most fertilizer manufacturers have now provided a product line that is suited specifically for vegetable gardens and chances are these will be available in the stores in your district. Spread the fertilizer over the entire surface of the garden and then begin the final preparations by raking it well into the soil.

Say you have made the soil physically ready for planting, all that remains to be done before seeding or transplanting is to rake and re-rake the surface until it becomes level and lump-free, with no high spots or hollows.

The Garden Layout

Because we are dealing with growing vegetables in somewhat difficult and crowded circumstances, the traditional garden layout may not make practical use of every available inch of space. With careful planning even a tiny growing space can be bountiful.

To get the best use out of limited growing space, first, be sure that your tall vegetables such as corn, beans, peas, staked tomatoes and other vine crops are planted on the north side of the garden where they will not cast shade on the other plants. Plan so that most of your climbing and vine crops can be grown tight against a wall or fence with all their growing parts well above the rest of the garden and taking up a minimum amount of surface space.

If you decide to try your hand at growing some of the spreading crops such as cucumbers, melons, squash and others (which may not be the best idea in a small space) remember that you can grow at least one crop of fast-growing, early vegetables from seed to maturity before other plants start spreading out and using that space. Your seed packages will tell you whether or not each kind of seed is an "early" variety, and how much time it will take to reach maturity.

In the crowded conditions we are discussing here, we *must* overlook the spacing directions on the seed packages. We cannot allow the plants the luxury of being six to twelve inches apart, if they will grow spaced at only four inches apart.

Beets normally are planted two inches apart in the row, with the rows spaced two feet apart. Here, we must bring the rows much closer together, to about eight inches apart.

Rows of beans, normally planted two feet apart, could be shrunk to rows only one foot apart, with each plant tied up to a wire or stake to grow on.

Cabbages are ordinarily planted two feet apart, in rows which are two feet from each other. Now we must bring the cabbages closer together, by a foot each way.

Use your own good judgment and common sense, but take a chance and grow your vegetables much closer together than normal. Keep the soil well-moistened to a good depth; keep out the weeds; supply only *slightly* more fertilizer than the instructions specify. Be sure to stop the applications of fertilizer on the dates recommended by the manufacturer. Cultivate often and keep the soil workable.

Whether you start with seeds sown in pots indoors or buy ready-grown transplants at planting time, don't skimp on quality. Buy the very best that you can afford. Seeding and transplanting suggestions are found elsewhere in this book.

Tomato plants can be trained in a wire cylinder.

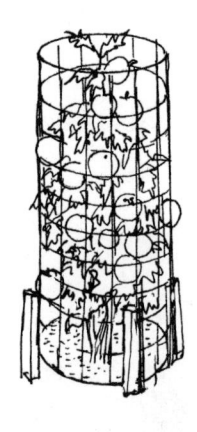

There are several vegetables that can and will produce more than one crop in one growing season. It is quite possible to have a non-stop supply of fresh, green onions from early spring to late fall. Start out by planting sets (bulbs), rather than seeds. Plant them two inches apart along a row. Two weeks later plant another row alongside, about six inches away from the first row planted. The first row of green onions will soon be ready for table use. You can then plant one more row, or sow seeds in the spaces that become available as you harvest the crop in the first row.

Try the same technique with seeds of carrots, radishes, beets, spinach, leaf lettuce, peas and others, and you'll be delighted at how much your bountiful little garden turns out. I suggest you keep on with this replacement-style planting until late in the season. The number of seeds that might be wasted would cost so little that you'd hardly notice the expense and you may be lucky during a mild autumn to reap an extra harvest.

Even in the coldest climate zones, home gardeners have found that they can dig up partly-grown Brussel sprouts, leaving a good soil ball at the root of the plants, and let them grow on to full maturity in a box in the garage, long after frost has killed everything else. There will be plenty of tricks you'll develop to help you utilize all the space at your disposal for the purpose of growing vegetables. The super-crowded conditions of Japan have forced home gardeners there to grow their vegetables in stacks of wooden boxes standing like the red squares of a vertical checker board.

An American gardener has built his own "tomato factory", a wooden box two feet square with an upright post at each corner. Four tomato plants are planted in the box and trained to climb the four uprights. This device produces more tomatoes than his family can consume in one summer. Such examples, of making a vegetable garden where it seemed impossible before, can be applied to the apartment balcony or to the crowded, downtown patio.

Have confidence and work hard. Cultivating a successful vegetable garden under adverse growing conditions will not be easy, but it can be done. Be prepared to give the project your attention and skill, and you will be rewarded with a generous supply of delicious, fresh vegetables.

HERB GARDENS

When a person is smitten with the compelling urge to make things grow, even under the most difficult conditions and in the smallest of spaces, he or she will eventually want to cultivate something that can be tasted as well as smelt and seen. Most often the size of the average garden limits the number of vegetables that can be grown. But even in the smallest plot of earth it is still possible to sow, grow, and harvest a crop of mealtime delights by planting your own herb patch.

Many herbs are beautiful to look at as well as to smell and taste— so much so, that they are often included in the flower beds and borders. Some herbs have rather untidy growing habits and should be planted in a secluded place away from public view. Most gardeners arrange things so that all the herbs are grown in the same garden patch where they compliment each other in a charming, rather old-worldish sort of way.

Some herbs are planted in the areas of the garden where the poorest soil is located. They will do reasonably well, but average soil with good drainage will yield the best results. Almost all herbs require full sunshine although they may have enough drought-resistance to tolerate very dry soil conditions.

The fragrance aspect of herb gardening is given best advantage when a sheltered location is chosen so that the four winds don't disperse the smells far and wide. You will want to keep those delightful scents confined. Snuggled into a fenced corner near a window is just about perfect for herbs as the fragrance will waft into the rooms. It may be best to choose a location that is nearest the kitchen so that you can dash out and pick a fresh leaf or two while the meal is being prepared.

The Three Main Kinds of Herbs

There are culinary herbs, medicinal herbs, and aromatic herbs: some are annual, biennial and perennial. Home gardeners are usually most interested in the culinary varieties that can be used to add zest to food.

ANNUAL HERBS Annual herbs should be sown directly outside in early spring (usually in May) in the place that has been set aside for them, as they do not transplant well. They have to grow and produce in one growing season. Some of the annual herbs for culinary use include: anise, basil, borage, chervil, summer savoury, and sweet marjoram. After the seedlings have sprouted and grown three or four inches, they may be thinned out to a spacing of four to five inches apart according to their mature size.

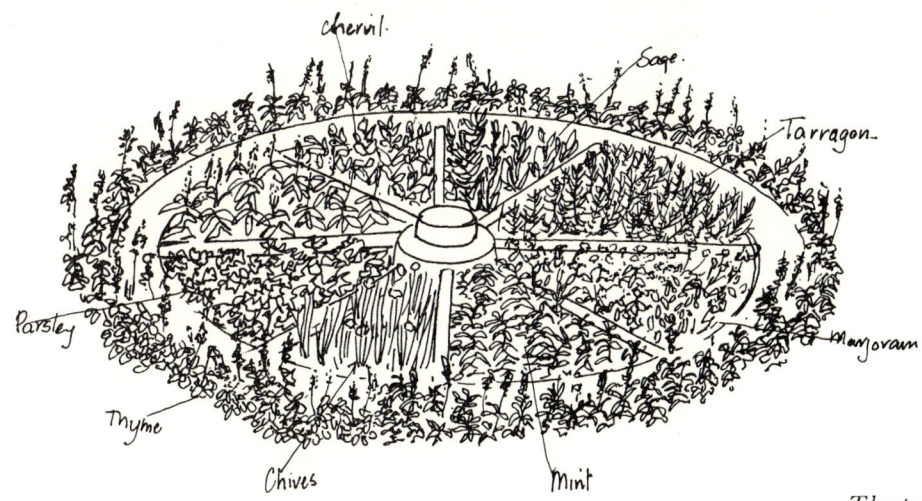

The traditional herb wagon wheel

PERENNIAL HERBS The seeds of perennial herbs should be sown about mid-May in a seedling bed and then transplanted to their permanent location when they are mature enough, sometime during the summer season. Horse radish, one of the most persistant perennial culinary herbs, does not transplant well and so should be sown where it is to grow permanently. Such herbs as mint, tarragon, and thyme are best grown from root divisions or cuttings (not from seed). Fennel is quite often grown as an annual although it may go dormant for the winter and regrow each year, as it is a perennial plant.

Some other herbs for culinary purposes which are perennial in habit include: chives; fennel; horse radish; mint; sage; tarragon; and thyme.

THE BIENNIAL HERBS Biennial plants are those that require two full seasons to produce a harvest—one season to establish roots and a second season to grow to maturity, then die.

Three common, biennial herbs for culinary purposes include: caraway; clary; and parsley. Parsley seeds should be sown in early spring and the plants kept through the winter either indoors, or in a protected cold frame. Caraway grows best from seed sown in early autumn. The crop can be harvested the following year. Clary seeds should be planted in July, transplanted in the fall, and the plants used the following summer.

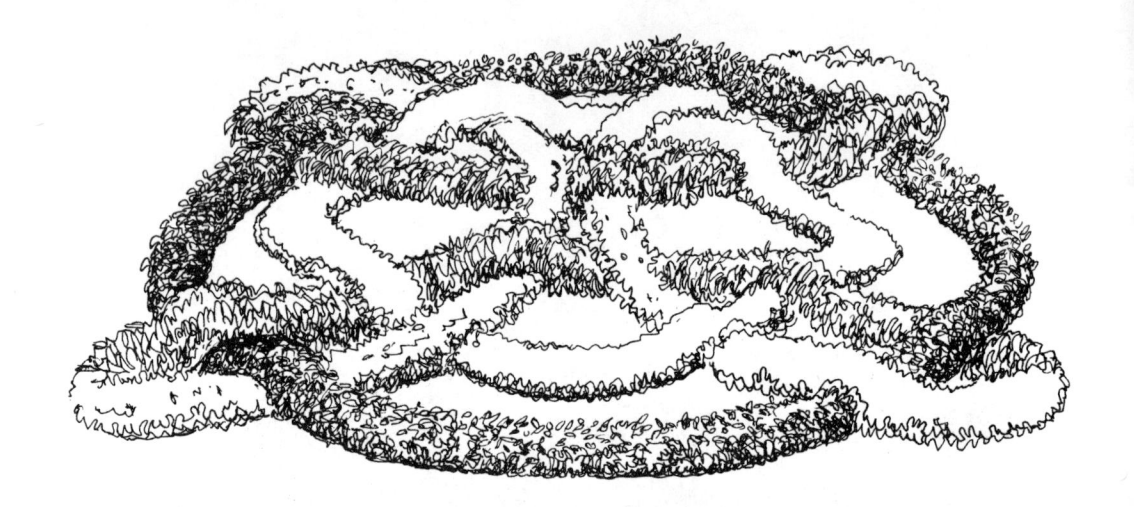

Many herb growers prefer the decorative knot garden.

Herb Garden Layouts

When the herb patch cannot be located near the kitchen door—handy for quick snips of this or that for the meal that's under preparation—then easy access to it might be by a stone path (or some form of pavement) to avoid wet or muddy feet.

WAGON WHEEL The wagon wheel layout is not only formal, but is almost a tradition with gardeners all over the world. A wagon wheel is laid flat on the ground and various herbs are planted around the rim and between the spokes in attractive patterns. Thyme makes a good edger around the wheel's rim, while other herbs are sparingly placed between the spokes including: chervil; chives; mint; sage; sweet basil; parsley; and tarragon; and if space is available, winter savory and sweet marjoram.

KNOT GARDEN Through the years the most spectacular herb displays have been created in the old-fashioned knot garden. The herbs are planted in a design that resembles a knotted rope. These so-called rope-knot gardens are made by weaving an intricate pattern of clipped herbs (mixed with small hedge shrubs) in the form of a continuous small, clipped hedge consisting of various colours and textures. The hedge twines and intertwines over and under itself to form the shape of a knot. The popular knot garden herbs include: lavender, mint, rue, thyme, and wormwood; hedge plants in the knot garden include boxwood and germander. These are often chosen because they are of compact growth habit and because of their tolerance of the drastic clipping which is necessary to maintain the shape required for the knot design.

When planted for household use and not for any sort of exhibition or display purpose, rectangular beds four feet wide with pathways in between are considered to be the most practical layout for the herb garden.

The traditional herb plant arrangements in the garden are many and varied and certainly always pleasing to the eye. You might try small beds at each corner of the patio or terrace, for example. These can be occupied by individual species of fragrant herbs while being, at the same time, handy to the kitchen. The onion-like flavour of chives can be picked from one corner, mint from another, parsley, dill, or caraway from other corners. There are many more herbs than corners and you find yourself looking for places where more herbs can be grown.

FALL FLOWERS

Each season o fthe year brings a stunning, colourful design all its own to the garden. Autumn can be considered to be a season of glorious colours displayed in the foliage of trees and shrubs. The numbers of daylight hours diminish and the leaves change their colours according to the amount of photosynthesis allowed them. But, even after the leaves have coloured-up and fallen from the branches and twigs, the garden can still offer a profusion of blazing colours because of the hardy, perennial plants.

Chrysanthemums

The chrysanthemums are considered to be one of the hardiest flowering plants and will often continue to display brilliant autumn colours even after light frosts have nipped many of the other garden flowers (usually most of the annuals). Chrysanthemums come in many different colours and sizes and can either be planted in permanent locations where their late-season colours will accent corners or you can buy fresh, already-flowering plants and place them anywhere in the garden.

Chrysanthemums, like most other perennial plants, need occasional lifting and dividing in order to keep the clumps looking and producing healthy and attractive blossoms. There are three basic methods of transplanting and dividing this plant, which are as follows:

(1) Leave a good soil ball on the roots at the time of digging. When they are being placed in the new location, be sure the soil is well-firmed around the plant, and then water well. The first winter the plants should be provided with a loose, protective mulch of straw, evergreen boughs or some such material in order to trap and hold as much snow as possible through the winter. (Snow is nature's finest insulation material.)

(2) After the first killing frost, dig up the plants, each with its shallow soil ball attached, and either place them in a cold frame for the winter, or in a flat in a storage area where the temperature never goes higher than 40 degrees. Apply water occasionally, but be sure that there is good drainage so that water will not linger to rot the roots.

(3) Chrysanthemum plants can also be brought through the winter in good condition for transplanting by digging the plants after a killing frost in the fall and setting them on the top of the soil. Mound soil around the entire plant and then cover with three or four inches of straw, or some other mulch material. With the arrival of warm spring weather, it is time to uncover, divide and replant the overwintered roots. When planted again they will provide a colourful show of flowers the following autumn.

Anemone Japonica

The graceful and beautiful *Anemone Japonica*, also known as the windflower, is another perennial plant that brings brilliance to the garden until the first frost arrives. Unquestionably, this delicate white, or rose-pink flower becomes a conversation-piece in the late fall flower garden, especially when planted in groups.

Provide this anemone with good drainage in rich, nutritious loam soil, that is open to sunshine and protected from strong winds. When this ideal situation can be had, you may get flowers the first year. The anemone may take up to four years to establish itself enough to produce the flowers, but believe me, the waiting is worthwhile.

Michaelmas Daisies

So large and varied is the number, of varieties of this plant that brightens the fall garden, that it is quite practical to plan an entire bed of Michaelmas daisies alone. There are dwarf, tall and medium forms in colours that range through white, pink, blue, red, and deep purple. Bloom begins in late summer and lasts right through the fall until a killing frost.

Also known as the fall aster, the Michaelmas daisy will bring, depending on how you group your plantings, either masses of colour or splashes of colour in your fall garden.

I have listed only three of the many plants that are available which will bring bright and pleasant colours to the garden in the autumn. A check of the plant lists and catalogues will soon supply names enough to fill a long list. You can surround yourself with wonderful colour if you make the effort to purchase plants that will banish the drabness that is usually associated with gardens in the fall of the year.

CUT & DRIED FLOWERS

Making things grow brings with it limitless thrills and pleasures, and is a vital link in the chain of man's survival on earth. One of the real assets of gardening is enjoying the harvest of fruits, vegetables, and flowers: particularly flowers when they are taken indoors and placed around in pleasing arrangements. In the very early spring, or late winter, we find ourselves forcing flowering bulbs into full bloom indoors, and we cut branches from flowering shrubs and coax them to flower in advance of the season. Our house plants also provide hours of pleasure by producing gorgeous flowers when the world outside is laden with ice and snow. With proper handling we can not only enjoy the glory of our own fresh-cut flowers during the flowering seasons, but we can also enjoy them months and even years later in the form of dried flowers.

Caring for Fresh-cut Flowers

Evening or early morning are preferred times for cutting flowers. If a container of water is carried with you to the garden and the flowers placed in the water immediately after cutting and then kept in a cool room for a few hours, flowers may be cut at any hour of the night or day. Either of the two above suggestions for the cutting of flowers will ensure the maximum length of freshness for your cut flowers.

How to Cut

When cutting flowers, be sure to use a good, clean, sharp knife or cutting shears, and make a slanting cut. In order to help supply the cut flower with needed nutrients, as many leaves as possible should be left on each stem. The wind and sun will reduce the quality of the flower when prolonged exposure is allowed, so keep them protected from the elements.

All cut flowers should be placed in cold water for no less than four hours to condition them before being set out in arrangements. Remove the lower leaves and place the container in a cool, dark, draft-free area. When this conditioning has been accomplished, the arrangements can be placed around the home to be given a change of water every day. Shorten stems about a half-inch at the same time.

When to Cut

Peonies and roses last longer when cut just as the outer petals are about to unfold.

Leave long stems on the dahlias and cut them before the blooms are completely open. Flower wilting can be prevented by cutting off an inch of the stems just prior to placing them in water.

Cut poppies the night they open, and place in water immediately.

Gladioli are best cut when one or two florets have opened on the spike. Insert a sharp, pointed knife into the stem, pierce it through and then bend the spike back and forth, and the stem will break at this point. Another cutting method is to slide the back of a sharp knife as far down the stalk as can be reached, then with feet placed at the base of the plant, draw the knife upward making a slanting cut. Always try to leave three or four leaves on the plant to manufacture food for the corm (the bulb).

Most flowers are best cut just before coming into full bloom. Annual flowers bloom profusely and recurrently, some of which make ideal cut flowers. Larger flowers can be encouraged when side buds along the branches are removed before they are fully developed. This transfers the plant's energy into the growth of the terminal buds at the tips of the branches.

Many gardeners have discovered the advantages of growing a flower garden just for cutting purposes only, usually in the vegetable garden, or behind a building and out of view.

Harvest Gourds and Herbs in the Fall

Gourds and herbs should be gathered and dried in September. Ornamental gourds are of no use as food and are used only as attractive, decorative ornaments, and in displays with other materials such as fruits, vegetables and cut flowers.

To dry gourds, leave them in the sun and give them an occasional turn to assure even drying on all sides. A soft brush, or the palm of your hand can be used to remove dirt and other unwanted material. Faster drying is encouraged by making a hole in the gourd with a darning needle. When thoroughly dried the gourds are left in their natural state, or given several coats of floor wax, or varnish, to prolong their appearance and make them glossy.

Drying Herbs

Some garden herbs may be past their best harvest time for drying purposes by September, while others are still quite useful. Large, coarse-leaved herbs should be allowed to dry in the sun for one or two hours after picking. After this period they should be hung in a well-ventilated room.

Herb seeds should be dried indoors for several days first, and then placed out in the sunshine for one or two days. When the leaves and seeds have dried they should be cleaned, separated from the stems and stored in airtight containers (jars). When stored in a darkened place such as a dark room or on a cupboard shelf, the leaf colour will last a longer period of time before fading.

Dried Flowers for Everlasting Bouquets

Arrangements of dried flowers have provided a uniquely-popular decorating touch for many years. It's just like having your living garden supplying colorful flowers any time you desire them. There are two basic methods of drying flowers and other garden produce, such as ornamental grasses, including the well-known air-drying method and one that requires silica gel crystals.

Air Drying

Cut the flowers before they reach full bloom as they will fully open during the stages of drying. After removing the foliage, tie the stems together, all heads pointing in the same direction, in small bunches. Hang them upside down in a well-ventilated, dark room. That's all there is to it. After drying, these dried flowers can be stored in boxes until required for indoor displays.

Some of the flowers that are known to be the easiest to dry include: Chinese lantern, cockscomb, and strawflowers (*Helichrysum*), among many others.

Other plants, many called weeds, also make good, dried materials for indoor displays in arrangements and groups. Sour dock, (the plant with the big, dark-brown seed capsules) and wild carrot, milkweed and thistle are also good plants to be collected and dried.

Some people prefer to gather and dry dozens of different forms of so-called wild plant material and then give them a spraying of gold, bronze, silver, or any other colour. The availability of paint in aerosol spray cans makes this work all the easier.

Silica Gel Crystals

Everlasting flowers for winter bouquets are often dried by means of a chemical called silica gel. Some of the flowers that dry better in this way, rather than by air drying, include: marigolds, roses, zinnias, and many different foliage plants.

A shoe box, or a metal cookie or candy tin make good containers as they can easily be made air-tight by taping the joints. Place a layer of silica gel in the bottom of the container to make it completely air-tight. On this layer place the flowers or foliage plants to be dried and gently cover them with more of the crystals. When the plant material is completely encased in the chemical, place the lid securely on the container and be sure it is made air-tight.

In about seven to ten days the plant material will be dry with colour and shape just as they were while growing in the garden. Store these dried specimens in an air-tight container where they'll be ready for instant use whenever the occasion arises.

The silica gel crystals can be reused after being dried out at 250 degrees Fahrenheit for 30 minutes in the oven.

If you have friends who are not familiar with dried flowers, or everlastings, you can astound them with displays of fresh-looking flowers months or even years after being cut from the garden. I have held seven-year-old flowers in my hand that could not be distinguished from flowers of the current year.

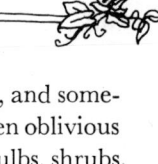

OVERRUN GARDENS

Oftentimes new-comers fall heir to an established, mature, and sometimes overgrown garden. The previous gardener may have been oblivious to the fact that he or she had planted too many perennials, bulbs, shrubs, or trees, perhaps simply because all the plants were small to begin with. Later, the effect is something like not being able to see the forest for the trees.

Perhaps every gardener should take a moment to stand back and have a good, long look at the object of his or her affection. It could be that it is time to do a little thinning out, trimming and transplanting to make the garden look less overgrown. When a garden has been allowed to become overcrowded and unruly, it will require a lot of work to get it back in presentable condition. Starting from scratch with a raw piece of rough ground to be turned into a landscape you can be proud of is easy compared to the planning and work required to renovate the older garden but rewards will come faster, and cheaper too, when you have established plants to work with or to move where you want them.

Don't Just Dig and Destroy

Resist the impulse to clear everything away and start fresh. The first thing you should *not* do is to dig haphazardly in with spade and fork and to toss everything out. A more practical plan is to leave the garden as is, making as few changes as possible until you know what is there.

A reliable way to go about finding out what grows where (and when) is to devise some sort of chart—a combination map-calendar—so that you can keep up to date on what is happening over the period of at least one year. The garden will likely take on noticeable changes in appearances approximately every two weeks. Chart the start of each plant's flowering by jotting down its location, size, colour, and whether or not it is overcrowded or can be dug up later and divided.

The Time to Dig

Mid-September is the time to follow through on your replanting scheme. Discard the plants that don't fit into your plan and set aside those you want to keep. In the meantime you can have ordered some of the new plants you may wish to bring into the landscape. (This particular move in itself will satisfy your almost-overwhelming desire to throw everything out and start fresh.) After you have devised a plan comes the creative part, which is easily one of the greatest thrills of gardening.

Most perennials can always be improved by being dug out and divided into smaller clumps. Those that bloom in the spring or early summer should be dug and divided in the fall; those that produce their flowers in the fall should be dug and divided in the spring. If you plan to revise an area that has been planted with a creeping, ground-covering plant variety, these plants may be lifted, divided and reset in the spring.

In any case, dig the soil well, add a complete fertilizer and some humus material before resetting perennial plants.

The Logic of the Plan

At the time you make general observations and note individual plant performances during the growing season, also make note of the ways in which the old-style garden fails to suit your modern way of living. This information, too, can be put to good use as the basis for the new plans you'll want to make.

In earlier times the style of planting was to plant everything away from the house so that the neighbours could see exactly what you had planted, and so that you could look out a window and survey your own domain from afar. The new-style-family trend is usually to keep the flowers up close to where life is really lived, right there on the patio or terrace area near the house.

Some particularly attractive specimens or groups of plants you may want to place in a location where they will disguise, hide, or perhaps emphasize a special feature of the overall scene: either improving it or screening it from view.

An open, airy, spacious effect is sometimes achieved when an overmature hedge is uprooted, or by the opening up of a nondescript overgrown border. The new plants' locations should provide perspective, be the right scale in relationship to the house, and feature growth habits that produce some special eye-appealing feature throughout each season of the year.

I feel it is a mistake, when renovating the older garden to eliminate all the old, traditional plants and replace them with the plant types and cultivars that have been developed for the modern setting. There could still be a place in your plans for such old-fashioned, fragrant plants as lilacs, herbs, spireas, clematis, shrub roses and peonies, among many others. When mixed in with the container-held, or potted contemporary plants (the succulents, cacti, crassulas, and aloes, and the other sun-worshipping plants such as geraniums and house plants that have a tolerance to sunshine and outdoor conditions) when combined with these, a beautiful blend of old charm and modern sophistication results.

Prune 'em Back Alive

When doing over the older garden, the shrubs and trees must be considered along with the flowering perennials and foliage plants. An orderly state can often be restored to an overgrown garden with some heavy pruning in the early spring before new growth begins. Most hedges may be cut to about twelve inches from the ground. Small trees and shrubs may be topped back and their lateral branches given a thinning and a shortening.

Those shrubs that grow in a clump formation and have developed weak and leggy canes and shoots will survive even when they are cut right back to ground level. It is sometimes a better procedure to cut out some of the heaviest and oldest canes at ground level allowing more light and space for development of the young growth.

One of the saddest sights in the old, mature garden is evergreens that have become shapeless and straggly, and on which the lower branches have become weak and thin. The garden would be better off without such sadly-neglected evergreens as, unfortunately, there is little chance that they can be rejuvenated. The junipers and cedars are usually the hardest hit in this way; when a yew (Taxus) is given an early spring pruning it will produce new growth from some of the mature wood.

When a shrub has been given a drastic pruning it will require from two to four years to come back to its original healthy form, but many times a more vigorous, healthy shrub is created because of the well-established root system. New growth can be speeded up by applying fertilizer around the shrubs at the time of pruning and then again in the spring of the following year.

Renewing shrub roses is handled in the same way as with other shrubs described above. For shrub roses and the climbers, the heavy, old canes should be cut out right at soil level to allow young shoots to develop faster. With roses, the times for such cutting-back work is either in the early spring or immediately after blooming.

LILACS NEW & OLD

Since the earliest days of pioneer life our homes and gardens have been graced with the beauty, charm and fragrance of lilacs. To this day, it is rare to discover a rural home that does not have a lilac border or wind screen somewhere near the building. Lilacs seem to simply go on and on without the need for any care or attention. In the rural setting this may be true of lilacs but where space is limited, as in the downtown garden, they must not be allowed to overgrow their allotted ground area.

Because the lilac is so common almost everywhere, even in the most severe, northern climate areas, one would almost consider the lilac to be a native of our country. This is not the case. The most common lilac, the French lilac, was obviously developed in France, while other varieties originated in Bulgaria and adjacent parts of Eastern Europe. Some came from Korea, Manchuria, Persia, the Himalayas and China, with the tree lilac coming from Japan.

The variety, of types of lilacs available, seems to be almost endless.

Dwarf Lilac

Not only are the new dwarf lilacs delightful specimens as solo plants or in the shrub border, they also form a distinctive hedge which won't exceed a height of four feet. During May and June the panicles of mauve flowers are backgrounded by dark-green foliage. The small plants form a compacted, rounded shape.

Where space is limited and the old charm of lilacs is desired, I highly recommend dwarf lilacs. When shopping for these plants make certain that the dwarfing feature has been verified.

Most Common Lilac

The French lilac, also considered to be the common variety, can be considered an asset to gardens of all sizes. Even though the common practice is to plant and forget lilacs, they somehow survive the neglect and continue to produce a crop of flowers every year, no matter what soil or location has been provided. It should also be noted that when given a little care and attention, such as good soil and occasional fertilizing, the common lilac will produce much larger and better quality flowers.

When and What To Plant

Lilacs should be planted in early spring, in a large hole filled with rich topsoil, or a mixture of topsoil, peat moss and leaf mold, with a five-inch flower-potful of (6–9–6) fertilizer added to the mix in each hole. The lilac plants should be set down a few inches deeper than the soil level at which they grew in the nursery and they should be given a good watering. (The previous depth of growth is easily seen as a collar mark on the bark.)

Visit a reliable nursery and purchase lilac plants that are two to three feet in height, and find out at the time of purchase whether or not the plants have been grafted. Some nurserymen have made some of the more exotic varieties possible to grow in the harsher climate areas by grafting them onto hardy privet stock. Grafted lilac plants must not be planted so deeply that the graft settles below the soil surface as the lilac stem will then form its own roots causing the privet root to die out (or else to grow its own shoots along with the lilac and need to be continually pruned out).

Some nurserymen of Europe are grafting lilacs onto seedlings of the common lilac (*Syringa vulgaris*) which must also be watched closely as the common lilac is apt to overgrow the desired cultivar which will not be what you want.

Care After Planting

Although it may be a tedious and tiresome task, all flowers should be removed from the plant right after they fade. Removing the faded flower heads (without removing any wood) helps produce bigger and better flowers for the next year as the shoots that will bear the next crop are forming at that time and they will benefit from the extra supply of growth energy that would have gone into seed production if the flowers had been left on the plant.

As much as those huge bouquets of lilacs with large woody stems are a delight to bring indoors in early summer, it is not wise to make such cuttings as the number of next year's flowers is thereby reduced. Cutting out the long stems with clusters of fragrant flowers is also cutting out many possible, future flower buds.

Some lilacs have the habit of quickly overgrowing and producing only a few flowers at the very tip of the tallest branches. This condition can be avoided by periodic renewal pruning. Maintain a balance between new and old growths. New shoots from ground level should be encouraged on young plants. Sometimes the new shoots on older plants become so crowded that only a few blooms are produced on a very unsightly plant. Generally speaking (and it is difficult to declare hard and fast rules) if you want to keep your lilacs at a height of ten feet or under, the older stems should be removed at soil level every second or third year. Thin out the new shoots according to the desired ultimate shape and height.

Care of Established Lilacs

When your established lilacs start producing inferior blooms it may be time for a rejuvenating program. This is accomplished by heavy pruning and by feeding.

Very old lilacs with many stems need to be reduced by fifty per cent at the soil level during the month of July. The next year, cut out the remaining fifty per cent of the old stems and thin out the new shoots that arise, leaving only four to six shoots to form a new plant. Then apply a good fertilizer (6-9-6) watered well into the soil.

When the plants are not too old, about one pound of 6-9-6 fertilizer should be spread on the soil around the plant and watered in every year, thus promoting vigorous growth.

By following these few simple suggestions, it is entirely possible for the gardener with the crowded downtown lot to enjoy the same benefits as the pioneers of our country and the royalty of Europe, by letting hardy, dependable lilacs bring their charms into the scene.